MODERN PATCHWORK

LEISURE ARTS, INC. • Maumelle, Arkansas

This book is filled with modern, contemporary projects of all kinds, including on-trend quilts, unique home décor projects, plus handy little totes, bags, and pouches to make your life easier. These 12 designs, from talented modern quilt designers, feature bold, high-contrast solid colors and prints, lots of negative space, and free-form quilting, and showcase the modern quilt movement.

FaveQuits.com is one of the 50 free cooking and crafting websites in the Prime Publishing community. FaveQuilts features thousands of free quilt patterns, tutorials, tips, articles, giveaways, and more. Their free, daily email newsletter, *Piecing It Together*, offers quilters inspiration with easy-to-follow patterns, tutorials, and gorgeous photos. FaveQuilts caters to quilters of all skill levels from those just starting out to those who have been quilting for decades. They are proud of the relationships they've built with hundreds of quilt bloggers and companies from around the world and are dedicated to bringing the best content to their loyal and dedicated fans.

The FaveQuilts community is flourishing all over social media from its nearly 100,000 Facebook fans to the 74,000 Pinterest followers to the dozens of tutorials available on their YouTube channel. The active online community allows quilters from all over the world to share what they're working on and receive feedback on their current projects. Quilters also have the opportunity to be published by submitting their original projects and images to the site. With over 30 new articles added to the site each week, there's no shortage of content for the quilting enthusiast to explore.

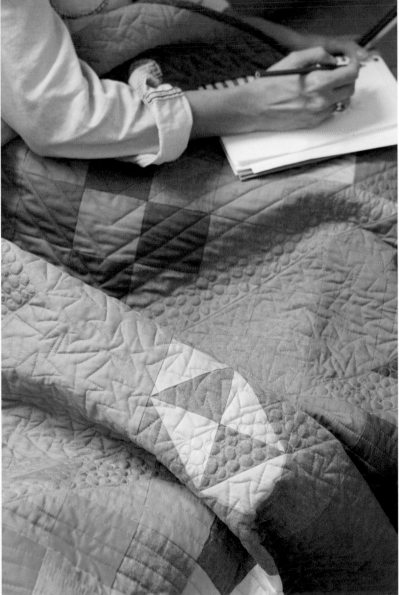

3

LINKED QUILT

DESIGN BY LINDSEY WEIGHT OF PRIMROSE COTTAGE QUILTS

QUILTING BY PRIMROSE COTTAGE QUILTS

This is a fast and easy quilt that uses strip piecing techniques. Blocks finish at 15" square so you can make your quilt as large or small as you want by adding or taking away blocks.

Finished Quilt Size: 63" x 63" (160 cm x 160 cm) | **Finished Block Size:** 15" x 15" (38 cm x 38 cm)

SHOPPING LIST

Yardage is based on 43"/44" (109 cm/112 cm) wide fabric with a usable width of 40" (102 cm).

- ☐ ⅝ yd (57 cm) of dark gray mottled print fabric
- ☐ 1 yd (91 cm) of light gray mottled print fabric
- ☐ 1⅜ yds (1.3 m) of pink mottled print fabric
- ☐ 2 yds (1.8 m) of white solid fabric
- ☐ ⅝ yd (57 cm) of fabric for binding
- ☐ 4 yds (3.7 cm) of fabric for backing

You will also need:
- ☐ 71" x 71" (180 cm x 180 cm) piece of batting

CUTTING THE PIECES

*Follow **Rotary Cutting**, page 58, to cut fabric. Cut all strips from the selvage-to-selvage width of the fabric. All measurements include ¼" seam allowances.*

From dark gray mottled print fabric:
- Cut 3 strips 5½" wide. From these strips, cut 16 **squares (A)** 5½" x 5½".

From light gray mottled print fabric:
- Cut 10 **(C) strips** 3" wide.

From pink mottled print fabric:
- Cut 5 strips 5½" wide. From these strips, cut 64 **rectangles (D)** 3" x 5½".
- Cut 5 **strips (E)** 3" wide.

From white solid fabric:
- Cut 10 **strips (B)** 3" wide.
- Cut 5 **strips (F)** 3" wide.
- Cut 6 strips 1½" wide. From these strips, cut 12 **sashing strips (G)** 1½" x 15½".
- Cut 5 **sashing strips (H)** 1½" wide.

From binding fabric:
- Cut 7 **binding strips** 2½" wide.

MAKING THE QUILT TOP

*Follow **Piecing**, page 59, and **Pressing**, page 60, to make quilt top. Use ¼" seam allowances throughout.*

1. Sew 1 **strip (B)** and 1 **strip (C)** together to make a **Strip Set A**. Press seam allowances toward the gray fabric. Make 10 Strip Sets. Cut Strip Sets into 64 Unit 1's 5½" x 5½".

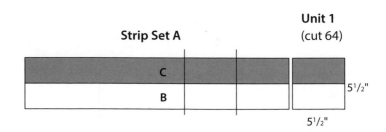

Strip Set A

Unit 1 (cut 64)

2. Sew 1 **strip (E)** and 1 **strip (F)** together to make a **Strip Set B**. Press seam allowances toward the pink fabric. Make 5 Strip Sets. Cut Strip Sets into 64 Unit 2's 3" x 5½".

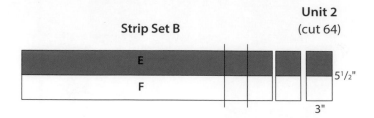

Strip Set B

Unit 2 (cut 64)

3. Sew 1 **rectangle (D)** to the bottom of 1 **Unit 2** to make a **Unit 3**. Press seam allowances toward the pink fabric. Make 64 Unit 3's. Each Unit 3 should measure 5½" x 5½".

Unit 3 (make 64)

4. Sew 2 Unit 3's and 1 Unit 1 together to make a Top Row. Press seam allowances toward Unit 3. Make 16 Top Rows.

Top Row (make 16)

5. Repeat Step 4 to make 16 Bottom Rows.

Bottom Row (make 16)

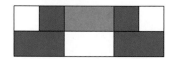

6. Sew 2 **Unit 1's** and 1 **square A** together to make a **Center Row**. Make 16 Center Rows.

Center Row (make 16)

7. Sew 1 Top Row, 1 Center Row, and 1 Bottom Row together to make a **Block**. Make 16 Blocks. Each block should measure 15½" x 15½".

Block (make 16)

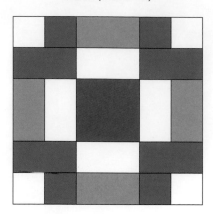

8. Sew 3 **sashing strips (G)** and 4 Blocks together to make 1 **Row**. Make 4 Rows.

9. Sew **sashing strips (H)** together end to end to make one long strip. Cut 3 long sashings 63½" long.

10. Refer to **Quilt Top Diagram** to sew 4 Rows and 3 long sashings together.

ASSEMBLING THE QUILT

1. Follow **Quilting**, page 60, to mark, layer, and quilt as desired. Quilt shown is quilted with diamonds turned on point.

2. Use binding strips and follow **Making Straight-Grain Binding**, page 62, to make binding. Follow **Attaching Binding with Mitered Corners**, page 62, to bind quilt.

Lindsey Weight would like to thank Riley Blake Designs for providing these beautiful fabrics.

Quilt Top Diagram

RAINBOW REFRACTION PILLOW

DESIGN BY ANN BUTLER DESIGNS

Using this easy strip-pieced technique, you'll have a pillow made in no time! To make your pillow even more unique, try sewing the strips together at angles. Or reverse the color placement. Use strips of white in the center and color on the outside edges for a completely different look.

Finished Pillow Size: approx. 15" x 13" (38 cm x 33 cm)

SHOPPING LIST

Yardage is based on 43"/44" (109 cm/112 cm) wide fabric with a usable width of 40" (102 cm).

☐ 1/8 yd (11 cm) *each* of pink, orange, yellow, teal, and purple solid fabrics
☐ 1 yd (91 cm) of white solid fabric

You will also need:

☐ two 20" x 20" (51 cm x 51 cm) pieces of low-loft batting
☐ polyester fiberfill

CUTTING THE PIECES

*Follow **Rotary Cutting**, page 58, to cut fabric. Cut all strips from the selvage-to-selvage width of the fabric. All measurements include 1/4" seam allowances.*

From *each* of the solid-color fabrics:

• Tear 3 strips 1" to 2 1/4" wide and 4 1/4" to 6 1/2" long.

From white solid fabric:

• Cut pillow back 20" x 20".
• Cut one 20" x 30" piece. From this piece, tear 6 strips 1" x 20" and 15 strips in widths to correspond with each colored fabric strip and 20" long. Tear these strips in half to make 10" strips.

MAKING THE PILLOW

*Follow **Piecing**, page 59, and **Pressing**, page 60, to make pillow. Use 1/4" seam allowances unless otherwise indicated.*

1. Sew short ends of 2 corresponding width 10" white solid strips to opposite ends of each colored strip. Repeat for all strips. Press seam allowances toward the color fabric.

2. Arrange strips as desired on 1 piece of batting (short ends do not have to be even), placing the six 1" x 20" strips between each color group and at the beginning and end (**Fig. 1**).

Fig. 1

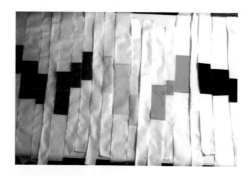

3. Working left to right, sew strips onto the batting in the order arranged. Begin by placing the first 2 strips, right sides together, on the left edge of the batting; sew. Press the strip open. Add the next strip, continuing across until all strips are sewn (**Fig. 2**).

Fig. 2

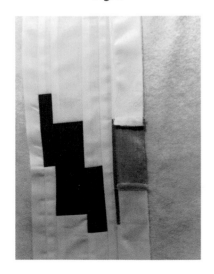

4. Trim pillow front to desired size (**Fig. 3**). My pillow front is trimmed 16" x 14". Trim the remaining batting and pillow back same size as pillow front.

Fig. 3

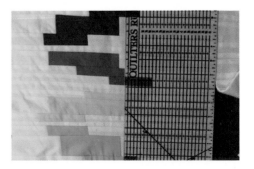

5. Place pillow back, right side up, on batting. Matching right sides, place pillow top on back.

6. Using a $1/2$" seam allowance, sew around the outer edge, leaving a 3" opening for turning. Turn the pillow right side out. Stuff pillow with fiberfill and stitch opening closed.

ASYMMETRICAL PLACE MATS

DESIGN BY CAROLINA MOORE

Make these simple modern place mats using half square triangles! Quick and easy to put together, once you have made one you can make another to match, or mix up your triangles to make a different modern design.

Finished Place Mat Size: 12" x 18" (30 cm x 46 cm)

SHOPPING LIST

Yardage is based on 43"/44" (109 cm/112 cm) wide fabric with a usable width of 40" (102 cm) and will make 1 place mat.

- ☐ ³/₄ yd (69 cm) of black solid fabric (includes backing and binding)
- ☐ ¹/₈ yd (11 cm) of blue solid fabric
- ☐ ¹/₈ yd (11 cm) of red solid fabric
- ☐ ¹/₈ yd (11 cm) of pink solid fabric

You will also need:

- ☐ 14¹/₂" x 20¹/₂" (37 cm x 52 cm) piece of batting
- ☐ water-soluble marking pen

CUTTING THE PIECES

*Follow **Rotary Cutting**, page 58, to cut fabric. Cut all strips from the selvage-to-selvage width of the fabric. All measurements include ¹/₄" seam allowances.*

From black solid fabric:

- Cut 1 strip 14¹/₂" wide. From this strip, cut 1 **backing** 14¹/₂" x 20¹/₂". From remaining fabric, cut 1 strip 12¹/₂" wide. From this strip, cut 1 **rectangle** 8" x 12¹/₂" and 1 **rectangle** 2" x 12¹/₂".
- Cut 2 **binding strips** 2¹/₂" wide.
- Cut 1 strip 2³/₈" wide. From this strip, cut 13 **squares** 2³/₈" x 2³/₈".
- Cut 1 strip 2" wide. From this strip, cut 1 **rectangle** 2" x 6¹/₂", 1 **rectangle** 2" x 5", 2 **rectangles** 2" x 3¹/₂", and 4 **squares** 2" x 2".

From blue solid fabric:

- Cut 1 strip 2³/₈" wide. From this strip, cut 9 **squares** 2³/₈" x 2³/₈".

From red solid:

- Cut 1 strip 2³/₈" wide. From this strip, cut 7 **squares** 2³/₈" x 2³/₈".

From pink solid fabric:

- Cut 1 strip 2³/₈" wide. From this strip, cut 7 **squares** 2³/₈" x 2³/₈".

MAKING THE PLACE MAT TOP

*Follow **Piecing**, page 59, and **Pressing**, page 60, to make quilt top. Use ¼" seam allowances throughout.*

1. Using the water-soluble marking pen, draw a line on the wrong side of the 2³/₈" pink square. Matching right sides, place the square on one 2³/₈" black square (**Fig. 1**).

2. Stitch ¼" on either side of the line (**Fig. 2**).

3. Cut on the drawn line to create 2 Half Square Triangles. Press the seam allowances toward the black fabric (**Fig. 3**).

4. Repeat to make the following combinations:
   - 2 additional squares pink with 2 additional squares black to make a total of 6 Half Square Triangles.
   - 5 squares red and 5 squares black to make 10 Half Square Triangles (only use 9)
   - 5 squares blue and 5 squares black to make 10 Half Square Triangles
   - 3 squares pink and 3 squares blue to make 6 Half Square Triangles
   - 1 square red and 1 square blue to make 2 Half Square Triangles (only use 1)
   - 1 square red and 1 square pink to make 2 Half Square Triangles (only use 1)

5. Refer to **Assembly Diagram** to lay out Half Square Triangles, black squares, and black rectangles.

6. Sew the pieces together in columns and sew the columns and large rectangles together.

ASSEMBLING THE PLACE MAT

1. Follow **Quilting**, page 60, to mark, layer, and quilt as desired. Place Mat shown is quilted with a diagonal grid of 2" squares in the large black rectangles, vertically in the ditch between the columns, and diagonally in the ditch through the Half Square Triangles.

2. Use binding strips and follow **Making Straight-Grain Binding**, page 62, to make binding. Follow **Attaching Binding with Mitered Corners**, page 62, to bind place mat.

Fig. 1

Fig. 2

Fig. 3

Assembly Diagram

Carolina Moore would like to thank Art Gallery Fabrics for providing these beautiful solid fabrics for her projects.

CROSSWEAVE TABLE RUNNER

DESIGN BY CAROLINA MOORE

This fun table runner looks like woven fabric. Even experienced quilters will wonder how it all came together — but by using a very simple partial seam, these blocks are a breeze!

Finished Table Runner Size: 12$\frac{1}{2}$" x 50" (32 cm x 127 cm)
Finished Block Size: 6$\frac{1}{4}$" x 6$\frac{1}{4}$" (16 cm x 16 cm)

SHOPPING LIST

Yardage is based on 43"/44" (109 cm/112 cm) wide fabric with a usable width of 40" (102 cm).

- ☐ $\frac{1}{8}$ yd (11 cm) of red solid fabric
- ☐ $\frac{1}{2}$ yd (46 cm) of white solid fabric
- ☐ $\frac{3}{8}$ yd (34 cm) of light blue solid fabric
- ☐ $\frac{3}{8}$ yd (34 cm) of dark blue solid fabric
- ☐ $\frac{3}{8}$ yd (34 cm) of fabric for binding
- ☐ 1$\frac{3}{4}$ yds (1.6 m) of fabric for backing

You will also need:

- ☐ 20" x 58" (51 cm x 147 cm) piece of batting

CUTTING THE PIECES

*Follow **Rotary Cutting**, page 58, to cut fabric. Cut all strips from the selvage-to-selvage width of the fabric. All measurements include $\frac{1}{4}$" seam allowances.*

From red solid fabric:
- Cut 1 strip 1$\frac{3}{4}$" wide. From this strip, cut 16 **squares** 1$\frac{3}{4}$" x 1$\frac{3}{4}$".

From white solid fabric:
- Cut 3 strips 4$\frac{1}{4}$" wide. From these strips, cut 64 **rectangles** 1$\frac{3}{4}$" x 4$\frac{1}{4}$".

From light blue solid:
- Cut 2 strips 4$\frac{1}{4}$" wide. From these strips, cut 32 **rectangles** 1$\frac{3}{4}$" x 4$\frac{1}{4}$".

From blue solid fabric:
- Cut 2 strips 4$\frac{1}{4}$" wide. From these strips, cut 32 **rectangles** 1$\frac{3}{4}$" x 4$\frac{1}{4}$".

From binding fabric:
- Cut 4 **binding strips** 2$\frac{1}{2}$" wide.

MAKING THE TABLE RUNNER TOP

*Follow **Piecing**, page 59, and **Pressing**, page 60, to make quilt top. Use ¼" seam allowances throughout.*

1. Sew 1 white solid rectangle and 1 dark blue rectangle together along 1 long edge. Press the seam allowances toward the dark blue fabric. Repeat to make a total of 32 white/dark blue rectangles and 32 white/light blue rectangles (**Fig. 1**).

2. Matching right sides, place a red square on top of the white rectangle on 16 white/light blue rectangles. Stitch half way down the red square; backstitch. Press the seam allowances toward the white fabric (**Fig. 2**). This is a partial seam and it will make it very easy to put the blocks together later.

3. With the white fabric along the upper edge, sew a white/dark blue rectangle on the unit just sewn along the entire edge. Press the seam allowances toward the white fabric. Repeat, moving **clockwise**, adding a white/light blue rectangle, then a white/dark blue rectangle. Finish the rest of the partial seam, stitching the open end of the seam closed as well as stitching over the previous stitches at least ¼" (**Fig. 3**). Repeat to make a total of 8 **Block A's**.

4. Repeat Steps 2-3, sewing the pieces together **counter-clockwise (Fig. 4)**. Repeat to make a total of 8 **Block B's**.

TABLE RUNNER TOP ASSEMBLY

1. Refer to **Table Runner Top Diagram** to sew the blocks together.

2. Follow **Quilting**, page 60, to mark, layer, and quilt as desired. Table Runner shown is quilted in the ditch between the pieces.

3. Use binding strips and follow **Making Straight-Grain Binding**, page 62, to make binding. Follow **Attaching Binding with Mitered Corners**, page 62, to bind quilt.

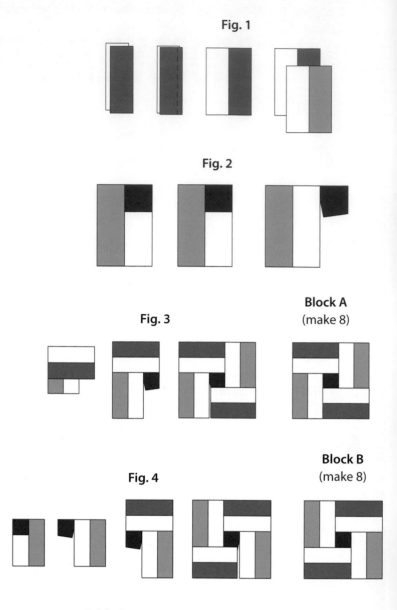

Fig. 1

Fig. 2

Fig. 3

Block A
(make 8)

Fig. 4

Block B
(make 8)

Table Runner Top Diagram

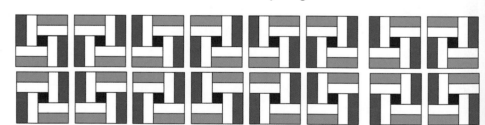

COLOR BLOCK PENCIL POUCHES

DESIGN BY CAROLINA MOORE

Use scraps from other projects in this book to make a fun and functional modern pencil pouch.

Finished Pouch Sizes: Small 3³/₄" x 7" (10 cm x 18 cm) and Large 4" x 8¹/₂" (10 cm x 22 cm)

SHOPPING LIST

A fat quarter measures approximately 18" x 21" (46 cm x 53 cm). Supplies given will make 1 pouch.

- ☐ scraps or fat quarters of 3 or more solid color fabrics
- ☐ one fat quarter of fabric for lining

You will also need:

- ☐ two 6" x 10" (15 cm x 25 cm) piece of fusible fleece
- ☐ 4" (10 cm) zipper

CUTTING THE PIECES

*Follow **Rotary Cutting**, page 58, to cut fabric. Cut all strips from the selvage-to-selvage width of the fabric. All measurements include ¹/₄" seam allowances.*

From scraps or fat quarters:
- Cut **strips** of varying widths and lengths. My strips varied from 1¹/₄" to 3³/₄" wide and were approximately 6" long.

From lining fabric:
- Cut 2 **linings** 4¹/₄" x 8" for small pouch **or** 4¹/₂" x 9" for large pouch.

MAKING A POUCH

*Follow **Piecing**, page 59, and **Pressing**, page 60, to make quilt top. Use ¹/₄" seam allowances throughout.*

1. Sew desired number of strips together to make 2 pieces at least 6" x 10". Press all the seam allowances in 1 direction. Fuse a piece of fusible fleece to the wrong side of each piece. From each piece, cut an outer pouch 4¹/₄" x 8" for small pouch **or** 4¹/₂" x 9" for large pouch (**Fig. 1**).

Fig. 1

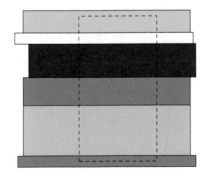

2. Place the zipper face down along the short edge of 1 lining piece (**Fig. 2**).

Fig. 2

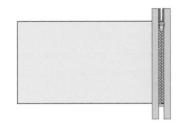

3. Place 1 of the outer pouch pieces on top, fusible fleece side up. Using a zipper foot, stitch along the edge of the zipper teeth (**Fig. 3**).

Fig. 3

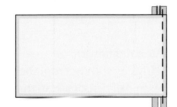

4. Matching wrong sides, fold the 2 pieces of fabric away from the zipper teeth, exposing the zipper; press (**Fig. 4**).

Fig. 4

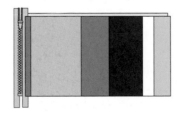

5. Repeat Steps 2-4 for the remaining outer pouch and lining pieces (**Fig. 5**).

Fig. 5

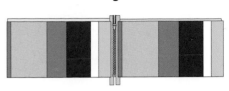

6. Open the zipper half way. Matching the right sides of the outer pouch pieces and the right sides of the lining pieces and with the zipper in the middle, sew the pieces together, leaving a 3"-4" opening for turning (**Fig. 6**). Be careful when sewing over the zipper.

Fig. 6

7. Trim the excess zipper ends and the corners. Turn the pouch right side out through the opening. Stitch the opening closed. Place the lining inside the pouch.

SQUARE DANCE QUILT

DESIGN BY CAROLINA MOORE

This bright and cheery quilt is simple to put together with 4 basic blocks that twist and turn to make fantastic secondary designs! Choose bright, bold colors for a fun statement quilt.

Finished Quilt Size: 48" x 48" (122 cm x 122 cm)
Finished Block Size: 6" x 6" (15 cm x 15 cm)

SHOPPING LIST

Yardage is based on 43"/44" (109 cm/112 cm) wide fabric with a usable width of 40" (102 cm).

- ☐ $7/8$ yd (80 m) of red solid fabric
- ☐ $1^3/8$ yds (1.3 m) of blue solid fabric
- ☐ $3/4$ yd (69 cm) of yellow solid fabric
- ☐ $1^1/4$ yds (1.1 m) of light gray solid fabric
- ☐ $1/2$ yd (46 cm) of fabric for binding
- ☐ $3^1/8$ yds (2.9 m) of fabric for backing

You will also need:

- ☐ 56" x 56" (142 cm x 142 cm) piece of batting
- ☐ water-soluble marking pen

CUTTING THE PIECES

Follow Rotary Cutting, page 58, to cut fabric. Cut all strips from the selvage-to-selvage width of the fabric. All measurements include $1/4$" seam allowances.

From red solid fabric:
- Cut 2 strips $3^7/8$" wide. From these strips, cut 16 **squares** $3^7/8$" x $3^7/8$".
- Cut 5 strips $3^1/2$" wide. From these strips, cut 48 **squares** $3^1/2$" x $3^1/2$".

From blue solid fabric:
- Cut 5 strips $6^7/8$" wide. From these strips, cut 24 squares $6^7/8$" x $6^7/8$". Cut these squares in half diagonally to make 48 **triangles**. From remaining fabric, cut 2 **squares** $3^7/8$" x $3^7/8$".
- Cut 2 strips $3^1/2$" wide. From these strips, cut 16 **squares** $3^1/2$" x $3^1/2$".

From yellow solid:
- Cut 2 strips $6^7/8$" wide. From these strips, cut 8 squares $6^7/8$" x $6^7/8$". Cut these squares in half diagonally to make 16 **triangles**.
- Cut 2 strips $3^7/8$" wide. From these strips, cut 14 **squares** $3^7/8$" x $3^7/8$".

From light gray solid fabric:
- Cut 10 strips $3^7/8$" wide. From these strips, cut 96 squares $3^7/8$" x $3^7/8$". Set aside 32 **squares**. Cut the remaining squares in half diagonally to make 128 **triangles**.

From binding fabric:
- Cut 6 **binding strips** $2^1/2$" wide.

GATHERING THE PIECES

Unit A

For *each* of 20 Unit A's, gather the following pieces:

- $6^{7}/_{8}$" blue triangle
- $3^{1}/_{2}$" red square
- $3^{7}/_{8}$" red square
- $3^{7}/_{8}$" light gray square
- two $3^{7}/_{8}$" light gray triangles

Unit B

For *each* of 28 Unit B's, gather the following pieces:

- $6^{7}/_{8}$" blue triangle
- $3^{1}/_{2}$" red square
- $3^{7}/_{8}$" yellow square
- $3^{7}/_{8}$" light gray square
- two $3^{7}/_{8}$" light gray triangles

Unit C

For *each* of 12 Unit C's, gather the following pieces:

- $6^{7}/_{8}$" yellow triangle
- $3^{1}/_{2}$" blue square
- $3^{7}/_{8}$" red square
- $3^{7}/_{8}$" light gray square
- two $3^{7}/_{8}$" light gray triangles

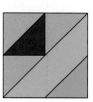

Unit D

For *each* of 4 Unit D's, gather the following pieces:

- $6^{7}/_{8}$" yellow triangle
- $3^{1}/_{2}$" blue square
- $3^{7}/_{8}$" blue square
- $3^{7}/_{8}$" light gray square
- two $3^{7}/_{8}$" light gray triangles

MAKING UNITS

*Follow **Piecing**, page 59, and **Pressing**, page 60, to make quilt top. Use $^{1}/_{4}$" seam allowances throughout.*

1. Using the water-soluble marking pen, draw a line on the wrong side of each $3^{1}/_{2}$" square and each $3^{7}/_{8}$" square (**Fig. 1**).

Fig. 1

2. Place one $3^{1}/_{2}$"square on the corner of one $6^{7}/_{8}$" triangle, Stitch on the line (**Fig. 2**). Trim seam allowances to $^{1}/_{4}$" (**Fig. 3**).

Fig. 2	**Fig. 3**

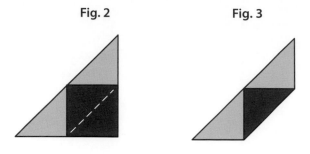

3. Open and press (**Fig. 4**). This is 1 half of the Unit.

Fig. 4

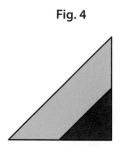

4. Place one $3^{7}/_{8}$" square on top of 1 light gray $3^{7}/_{8}$" square (**Fig. 5**).

Fig. 5

5. Stitch $^{1}/_{4}$" on either side of the line (**Fig. 6**). Cut along the drawn line.

Fig. 6

6. Open and press the Half Square Triangle (**Fig. 7**). Clip the dog ears. Set 1 aside for making another unit.

Fig. 7

7. Sew a light gray triangle to 1 side of the Half Square Triangle (**Fig. 8**). Open and press. Clip the dog ears.

Fig. 8

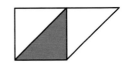

8. Repeat, adding a light gray triangle to the adjacent side (**Fig. 9**). Open and press. Clip the dog ears. This is the second half of the Unit.

Fig. 9

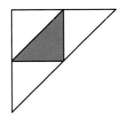

9. Place the 2 halves right sides together. Stitch along the long edge. Open and press (**Fig. 10**).

Fig. 10

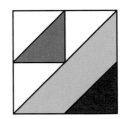

10. Repeat Steps 2-9, making a total of 20 Unit A's, 28 Unit B's, 12 Unit C's, and 4 Unit D's.

Quilt Top Assembly

1. Refer to **Quilt Top Diagram** to sew the Units into Rows and the Rows together.

2. Follow **Quilting**, page 60, to mark, layer, and quilt as desired. Quilt shown is quilted with diagonal lines across the quilt.

3. Use binding strips and follow **Making Straight-Grain Binding**, page 62, to make binding. Follow **Attaching Binding with Mitered Corners**, page 62, to bind quilt.

Quilt Top Diagram

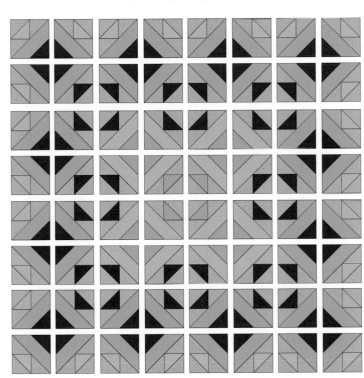

IRON BAG

DESIGN BY BECKY JORGENSEN

The pack and go bag is designed so you can carry your iron to and from sewing class and quilting circles, even while it's still hot! This pattern offers a simple template with an optional appliqué so you can create your own in a retro bowling bag style.

Finished Bag Size: 11" x 8" (28 cm x 20 cm), excluding handles

SHOPPING LIST

Yardage is based on 43"/44"
(109 cm/112 cm) wide fabric with a
usable width of 40" (102 cm).

- ☐ ½ yd (46 cm) of pink print fabric for outer bag and handles
- ☐ ³/₈ yd (34 cm) of fabric for lining
- ☐ ³/₈ yd (34 cm) of purple solid fabric for appliqués and button flap
- ☐ ⅛ yd (11 cm) of orange solid fabric for piping

You will also need:

- ☐ 32" x 12" (81 cm x 30 cm) piece of The Warm Company® Insul-Brite™ needle-punched insulated lining or sew-in fleece
- ☐ 2³/₄ yds (2.5 m) of ¹/₁₆" (1.6 mm) diameter cord for piping
- ☐ 1⅛" (29 mm) diameter button

CUTTING THE PIECES

*Follow **Rotary Cutting**, page 58, to cut fabric. Cut all strips from the selvage-to-selvage width of the fabric. All measurements include ¼" seam allowances.*

From fabric for outer bag and handles:
- Use pattern, page 57, to cut 2 **outer bags**.
- Cut 4 **handles** 2½" x 10".

From fabric for lining:
- Use pattern, page 57, to cut 2 **bag linings**.

From fabric for appliqué and button flap:
- Use pattern, page 56, to cut 2 **appliqués**; cut 2 appliqués in reverse.
- Cut 2 **button flaps** 3" x 3".

From fabric for piping:
- Cut 3 strips 1" x width of fabric. Joint strips together and cut 1" x 99" **piping strip**.

From insulated lining or sew-in fleece:
- Use pattern, page 57, to cut 2 **outer bags**.
- Cut **button flap** 3" x 3".
- Cut 2 **handles** 2½" x 10".

MAKING THE BAG

*Follow **Piecing**, page 59, and **Pressing**, page 60, to make bag. Use ¼" seam allowances unless otherwise indicated.*

Adding the Appliqués

1. Fold piping strip in half lengthwise, sandwiching piping cord in between at the fold. Using a zipper foot, sew close to the cord **(Fig. 1)**. Cut four 10" lengths and four 13" lengths.

2. Matching right sides and raw edges, lay 1 longer piping along the longer edge of the appliqué. Using a zipper foot, sew close to the cord. Repeat with 1 shorter piping along the shorter edge of the appliqué (**Fig. 2**). Press the seam allowances to the wrong side.

3. Repeat Step 2 to make 3 additional appliqués.

4. Place 1 outer bag on top of an insulated lining bag. Pin the appliqué in place as shown on pattern. Sew along the appliqué edge (**Fig. 3**). This will secure the fleece and create a quilted effect.

5. Repeat Step 4 to attach another appliqué to this outer bag and to add the remaining appliqués to the remaining outer bag.

Fig. 1

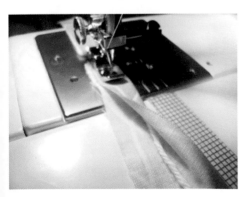

Fig. 2

Fig. 3

Adding the Button Flap

1. Matching right sides, place 2 button flaps together; place them on top of the insulated lining button flap. Sew around 3 sides, leaving 1 side (top) open for turning **(Fig. 4)**. Trim the corners. Turn the flap right side out; press.

2. Make a buttonhole about $1/2$" from 1 edge and centered on the flap. Be sure to check your button size!

3. Matching top raw edges, pin the flap to 1 outer bag, centered between 2 appliqués. Stitch $1/8$" from top edge **(Fig. 5)**.

Adding the Handles

1. Matching right sides, place 2 handles together; place them on top of the insulated lining handle. Sew along each long side. Turn the handle right side out; press.

2. Topstitch $1/4$" from each long edge of each handle.

3. Matching raw edges, pin 1 handle to 1 outer bag, centered on the appliqués. Stitch $1/8$" from ends of handles **(Fig. 6)**.

4. Repeat Steps 1-3 to make and attach another handle.

Fig. 4

Fig. 5

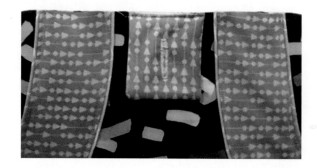

Fig. 6

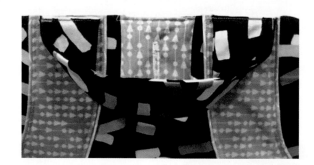

ASSEMBLING THE BAG

1. Matching right sides and keeping handles tucked inside, place 2 outer bags together.

2. Using the pattern, mark the outer bag with a pin on each side where sewing will start and stop. Beginning at 1 pin, sew down 1 side, across the bottom, and up the other side, stopping at the pin (**Fig. 7**).

3. To box each corner, pinch the bottom corners to flatten them. Draw a line 1¹/₂" from the tip. Sew across the tip as shown in **Fig. 8**. Cut off excess to reduce bulk. Turn right side out.

4. Repeat Steps 2-3 with bag lining, leaving a 3" opening along the bottom for turning.

5. Matching right sides, place the outer bag inside the bag lining; pin the sides and along the top.

6. Realigning fabrics as needed, sew along the top and sides of the bag. As you reach the side seams, stop with needle down, pivot the bag, sew across the side seam, pivot the bag again, and continue around top of bag (**Fig. 9**).

7. Turn the bag right side out through the opening in the bottom of the lining. Hand stitch the opening closed.

8. Place the lining inside the bag and press the top edge. Topstitch ¹/₄" from the top edge of the bag, pivoting and turning in the same manner as previous (**Fig. 10**)

9. Mark button placement and sew button in place.

Fig. 7

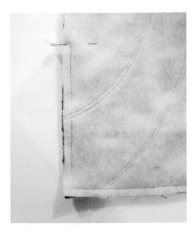

Fig. 8

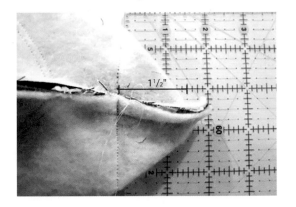

Fig. 9

Fig. 10

CULINARY BRIGHTS APRON

DESIGN BY MARY BETH TEMPLE

Use precut fabrics or your own stash to make this quick and easy apron.

Finished Apron Size: 32¹/₂" x 20" (83 cm x 51 cm)

SHOPPING LIST

Yardage is based on 43"/44" (109 cm/112 cm) wide fabric with a usable width of 40" (102 cm). A fat quarter measures approximately 18" x 21" (46 cm x 53 cm).

☐ 3 matching fat quarters *or* 2 matching 18" x 21" (46 cm x 53 cm) pieces of fabric for apron skirt and pocket lining

☐ 2 sets of 2 matching jelly roll strips *or* 2 sets of 2 matching strips 2¹/₂" x 40" (6 cm x 102 cm) strips for tie

☐ 3 assorted charm squares *or* 3 assorted squares 5" x 5" (13 cm x 13 cm) for pockets

☐ 36 assorted mini charm squares *or* 36 assorted squares 2¹/₂" x 2¹/₂" (6 cm x 6 cm) for pockets

MAKING THE APRON

*Follow **Piecing**, page 59, and **Pressing**, page 60, to make apron. Use ¹/₄" seam allowances unless otherwise indicated.*

Skirt

1. For flat center seam, match **wrong** sides and use a ¹/₂" seam allowance to sew long edges of 2 fat quarters together. Trim away about ¹/₂ of 1 seam allowance. Press the remaining seam allowance in half to wrong side and then press the folded seam allowance over the trimmed seam allowance. Topstitch in place along the folded edge.

2. For side hem, press 1 short edge ¹/₄" to wrong side; press 1" to wrong side again. Stitch along inner folded edge. Repeat for remaining side hem.

3. For bottom hem, press 1 long edge ¹/₂" to wrong side; press 2" to wrong side again. Stitch along inner folded edge.

4. Stitch a long basting stitch ³/₈" from raw edge; stitch another long basting stitch ¹/₄" from raw edge. Set skirt aside.

Tie

1. Sew each pair of strips together along 1 short edge; press seam allowances open.

2. Matching right sides, pin strips together along long edges.

3. Trim each end diagonally at a 45° angle.

4. Sew strips together, leaving 9" to either side of the center seam open.

5. Clip corners, turn right side out, and press, pressing under the seam allowances at the opening. Set tie aside.

Pocket

1. Trim each charm square to 4¹/₂" x 4¹/₂" for block center.

2. Arrange 12 mini charm squares as desired around charm square.

3. Sew 2 mini charm squares together to make **Unit 1**; press seam allowances to 1 side. Repeat to make a total of 2 Unit 1's.

4. Sew Unit 1's to top and bottom of block center; press seam allowances away from the block center.

5. Sew 4 mini squares together to make **Unit 2**; press seam allowances to 1 side. Repeat to make a total of 2 Unit 2's.

6. Sew 1 Unit 2 to each side of the block center; press seam allowances away from the block center.

7. Repeat Steps 2-6 to make a total of 3 pockets.

8. Sew pockets together side by side. Set pockets aside.

Pocket Lining

1. Cut remaining fat quarter into 2 pocket linings 8¹/₂" x 12¹/₂".

2. Sew the pocket linings together along 1 short edge; press seam allowances open.

3. With right sides facing, sew pocket to pocket lining, leaving an opening for turning.

4. Clip corners, turn right side out and press, pressing under the seam allowances at the opening.

Finishing

1. Center and pin the pocket 3" above the bottom hem, with the open edge at the bottom.

2. Topstitch the pocket in place along 2 sides and the bottom.

3. Topstitch in the ditch between each block to form 3 pockets.

4. Use basting threads to gather the apron top to 18".

5. Pin gathered apron top into bottom opening of tie, spreading the gathers evenly.

6. Topstitch all the way around the tie, beginning and ending at 1 angled end. Trim all threads.

Unit 1 (make 2)

Unit 2 (make 2)

Pocket (make 3)

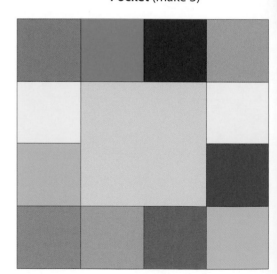

COLOR-BLOCKED TOTE

DESIGN BY ALICIA STEELE

You can never have enough tote bags! Whether carrying your supplies to your next quilting class or to the market, this tote will handle it all!

Finished Tote Size: 11½" x 17¾" (29 cm x 45 cm) excluding handles

SHOPPING LIST

Yardage is based on 43"/44" (109 cm/112 cm) wide fabric with a usable width of 40" (102 cm).

- ☐ ¾ yd (69 cm) of white solid fabric
- ☐ ⅝ yd (57 cm) of blue solid fabric
- ☐ ⅛ yd (11 cm) of teal solid fabric
- ☐ ⅛ yd (11 cm) of pink solid fabric

You will also need:

- ☐ 18½" x 24½" (47 cm x 62 cm) piece of fusible fleece
- ☐ walking foot for sewing machine

CUTTING THE PIECES

*Follow **Rotary Cutting**, page 58, to cut fabric. Cut all strips from the selvage-to-selvage width of the fabric. All measurements include ¼" seam allowances.*

From white solid fabric:
- Cut 1 strip 8½" wide. From this strip, cut 1 **rectangle (C)** 8½" x 7½", 2 **rectangles (A & J)** 5½" x 8½", and 2 **rectangles (B & K)** 2½" x 8½".

- Cut 1 strip 4½" wide. From this strip, cut 1 **rectangle (O)** 3½" x 4½" and 2 **rectangles (G & N)** 2½" x 4½". From remainder of strip, cut 1 strip 2½" wide. From this strip, cut 3 **squares (E, L, & R)** 2½" x 2½".

- Cut 4 strips 2" wide. From these strips, cut 4 **handles** 2" x 22".

- Cut 1 strip 1½" wide. From this strip, cut 1 **rectangle (V)** 1½" x 16½", 1 **rectangle (T)** 1½" x 6½", and 1 **rectangle (P)** 1½" x 4½".

From blue solid fabric:
- Cut 1 strip 18½" wide. From this strip, cut 1 **lining rectangle** 24½" x 18½" and 1 **rectangle (D)** 8½" x 10½".

From teal solid fabric:
- Cut 1 strip 3½" wide. From this strip, cut 1 **rectangle (S)** 3½" x 24½", 1 **square (Q)** 2½" x 2½", and 1 **rectangle (U)** 1½" x 2½".

From pink solid fabric:
- Cut 1 strip 2½" wide. From this strip, cut 2 **rectangles (H & I)** 2½" x 8½" and 2 **squares (F & M)** 2½" x 2½".

MAKING THE TOTE

*Follow **Piecing**, page 59, and **Pressing**, page 60, to make quilt top. Use ¼" seam allowances throughout.*

1. Refer to the **Tote Body Diagram** to sew pieces together in the following order. ***Note:*** *When more than 2 pieces of fabric have been joined, the middle letters will be dropped to help avoid confusion.*

- Sew **E**, **F**, and **G** together.
- Sew **A** to **E-G**.
- Sew **A-G** to **H**.
- Sew **A-H** to **J**.
- Sew **B**, **D** and **K** together.
- Sew **C** to **I**.
- Sew **L**, **M**, and **N** together.
- Sew **CI** to **L-N**.
- Sew **Q** to **R**.

- Sew **QR** to **P**.
- Sew **P-R** to **O**.
- Sew **C-N** to **O-R**.
- Sew **T**, **U**, and **V** together.
- Sew **T-V** to **S**.
- Sew **A-J** to **B-K**.
- Sew **A-K** to **C-R**.
- Sew **A-R** to **S-V**.

Tote Body Diagram

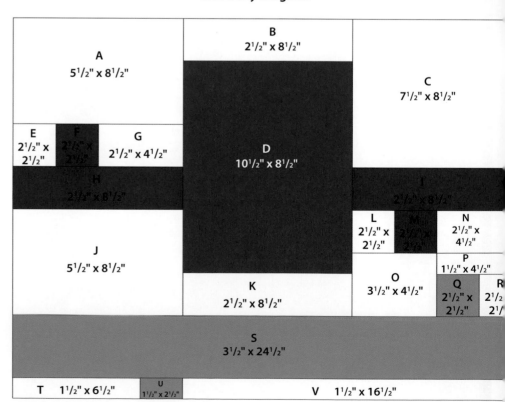

2. Follow manufacturer's instructions to fuse fleece to the wrong side of the pieced tote body.

3. Use a walking foot to quilt through the tote body and fleece as desired. Stitch straight lines in the ditch and a few straight lines along the piece.

4. Matching right sides and short edges, fold the quilted tote body in half. Make sure the pink and teal seamlines match along the raw edge. Sew along the side and bottom edges; turn piece right side out.

5. Match right sides and sew the lining rectangle together along long raw edges. This creates a tube.

6. Matching right sides, place the tote body in the lining tube. Sew the top raw edge of the lining to the top raw edge of the tote body.

7. Turn the tube right side out. This will bring the tote body to the outside.

8. Press the open lining edge to wrong side ¼" and sew closed with a straight stitch. Place the lining inside the tote body. Don't place the lining all the way into the tote body. Press the upper edge of the lining so that desired amount of lining is showing at top of tote body.

9. To make 1 handle, match right sides and sew 2 handles together along the 2 long edges and 1 short edge. Repeat with the remaining handles. **Optional:** You can add a 1½" wide strip of fusible fleece to the handle for padding.

10. Turn the handles right side out and press the short raw edges under ¼".

11. Pin the finished end of 1 handle on the outside and the pressed end on the inside. Sew the handle in place by making a square and then draw an X through the square. Repeat with the remaining handle, making sure to align the second handle with the first handle.

OMBRÉ PATCHWORK QUILT

DESIGN BY KIM LAPACEK
QUILTING BY KIM VAN ETTEN

Finished Quilt Size: 60" x 72" (152 cm x 183 cm)

SHOPPING LIST

*Yardage is based on 43"/44"
(109 cm/112 cm) wide fabric with a
usable width of 40" (102 cm).*

- ☐ ³/₄ yd (69 cm) *each* of 8 assorted gray solid fabrics in different values from light to dark for the background
- ☐ ³/₈ yd (34 cm) of indigo ombré fabric
- ☐ ³/₈ yd (34 cm) of purple ombré fabric
- ☐ ¹/₄ yd (23 cm) of hot pink ombré fabric
- ☐ ¹/₄ yd (23 cm) of avocado ombré fabric
- ☐ ¹/₄ yd (23 cm) of mustard ombré fabric
- ☐ ³/₈ yd (34 cm) of magenta ombré fabric
- ☐ ¹/₄ yd (23 cm) of persimmon ombré fabric
- ☐ ³/₈ yd (34 cm) of teal ombré fabric
- ☐ ⁵/₈ yd (57 cm) of fabric for binding
- ☐ 4¹/₂ yds (4.1 m) of fabric for backing

You will also need:
- ☐ 68" x 80" (173 cm x 203 cm) piece of batting

CUTTING THE PIECES

*Follow **Rotary Cutting**, page 58, to cut fabric. Cut all strips from the selvage-to-selvage width of the fabric. All measurements include ¹/₄" seam allowances.*

From gray solid fabric #1 (lightest):
- Cut 1 strip 9¹/₂" wide. From this strip, cut 2 **rectangles** 6¹/₂" x 9¹/₂", 1 **rectangle** 9¹/₂" x 12¹/₂", 1 **rectangle** 3¹/₂" x 9¹/₂", and 1 **square** 4" x 4".
- Cut 2 strips 3¹/₂" wide. From these strips, cut 17 **squares** 3¹/₂" x 3¹/₂".

From gray solid fabric #2:
- Cut 1 strip 9¹/₂" wide. From this strip, cut 3 **rectangles** 6¹/₂" x 9¹/₂" and 2 **rectangles** 3¹/₂" x 9¹/₂".
- Cut 2 strips 3¹/₂" wide. From these strips, cut 2 **rectangles** 3¹/₂" x 6¹/₂" and 13 **squares** 3¹/₂" x 3¹/₂".
- Cut 1 strip 4" wide. From this strip, cut 4 **squares** 4" x 4".

From gray solid fabric #3:
- Cut 1 strip 9¹/₂" wide. From this strip, cut 2 **rectangles** 9¹/₂" x 6¹/₂" and 3 **rectangles** 9¹/₂" x 3¹/₂".
- Cut 2 strips 3¹/₂" wide. From these strips, cut 16 **squares** 3¹/₂" x 3¹/₂" and 2 **rectangles** 3¹/₂" x 6¹/₂".
- Cut 1 strip 4" wide. From this strip, cut 6 **squares** 4" x 4".

From gray solid fabric #4:
- Cut 1 strip 6¹/₂" wide. From this strip, cut 2 **rectangles** 6¹/₂" x 9¹/₂".
- Cut 3 strips 3¹/₂" wide. From these strips, cut 3 **rectangles** 3¹/₂" x 9¹/₂", 2 **rectangles** 3¹/₂" x 6¹/₂", and 13 **squares** 3¹/₂" x 3¹/₂".
- Cut 2 strips 4" wide. From these strips, cut 10 **squares** 4" x 4".

From gray solid fabric #5:
- Cut 1 strip 9¹/₂" wide. From this strip, cut 2 **rectangles** 6¹/₂" x 9¹/₂", 1 **rectangle** 9¹/₂" x 12¹/₂", and 1 **rectangle** 3¹/₂" x 9¹/₂".
- Cut 2 strips 3¹/₂" wide. From these strips, cut 2 **rectangles** 3¹/₂" x 6¹/₂" and 14 **squares** 3¹/₂" x 3¹/₂".
- Cut 1 strip 4" wide. From this strip, cut 3 **squares** 4" x 4".

From gray solid fabric #6:
- Cut 1 strip 9¹/₂" wide. From this strip, cut 2 **rectangles** 6¹/₂" x 9¹/₂" and 3 **rectangles** 3¹/₂" x 9¹/₂".
- Cut 2 strips 3¹/₂" wide. From these strips, cut 2 **rectangles** 3¹/₂" x 6¹/₂" and 15 **squares** 3¹/₂" x 3¹/₂".
- Cut 1 strip 4" wide. From this strip, cut 5 **squares** 4" x 4".

From gray solid fabrics #7:
- Cut 1 strip 9¹/₂" wide. From this strip, cut 1 **rectangle** 9¹/₂" x 12¹/₂", 2 **rectangles** 9¹/₂" x 6¹/₂" and 1 **rectangle** 9¹/₂" x 3¹/₂".
- Cut 2 strips 3¹/₂" wide. From these strips, cut 3 **rectangles** 3¹/₂" x 6¹/₂" and 13 **squares** 3¹/₂" x 3¹/₂".
- Cut 1 strip 4" wide. From this strip, cut 2 **squares** 4" x 4".

From gray solid fabric #8 (darkest):
- Cut 1 strip 9¹/₂" wide. From this strip, cut 2 **rectangles** 6¹/₂" x 9¹/₂" and 3 **rectangles** 3¹/₂" x 9¹/₂".
- Cut 2 strips 3¹/₂" wide. From these strips, cut 1 **rectangle** 3¹/₂" x 6¹/₂" and 16 **squares** 3¹/₂" x 3¹/₂".
- Cut 1 strip 4" wide. From this strip, cut 3 **squares** 4" x 4".

From indigo ombré fabric:
- Cut 2 strips 3¹/₂" wide. From these strips, cut 14 **squares** 3¹/₂" x 3¹/₂".
- Cut 1 strip 4" wide. From this strip, cut 3 **squares** 4" x 4".

From purple ombré fabric:
- Cut 2 strips 3¹/₂" wide. From these strips, cut 14 **squares** 3¹/₂" x 3¹/₂".
- Cut 1 strip 4" wide. From this strip, cut 2 **squares** 4" x 4".

From hot pink ombré fabric:
- Cut 1 strip 3¹/₂" wide. From this strip, cut 14 **squares** 3¹/₂" x 3¹/₂".
- Cut 1 strip 4" wide. From this strip, cut 4 **squares** 4" x 4".

From avocado ombré fabric:
- Cut 1 strip 3¹/₂" wide. From this strip, cut 6 **squares** 3¹/₂" x 3¹/₂".
- Cut 1 strip 4" wide. From these strips, cut 10 **squares** 4" x 4".

From mustard ombré fabric:
- Cut 1 strip 3¹/₂" wide. From this strip, cut 9 **squares** 3¹/₂" x 3¹/₂".
- Cut 1 strip 4" wide. From this strip, cut 1 **square** 4" x 4".

From magenta ombré fabric:
- Cut 2 strips 3¹/₂" wide. From this strip, cut 4 **squares** 3¹/₂" x 3¹/₂".
- Cut 1 strip 4" wide. From this strip, cut 4 **squares** 4" x 4".

From persimmon ombré fabric:
- Cut 1 strip 3¹/₂" wide. From this strip, cut 11 **squares** 3¹/₂" x 3¹/₂".
- Cut 1 strip 4" wide. From this strip, cut 6 **squares** 4" x 4".

From teal ombré fabric:
- Cut 2 strips 3¹/₂" wide. From these strips, cut 22 **squares** 3¹/₂" x 3¹/₂".
- Cut 1 strip 4" wide. From this strip, cut 4 **squares** 4" x 4".

From binding fabric:
- Cut 8 **binding strips** 2¹/₂" wide.

MAKING THE QUILT TOP

*Follow **Piecing**, page 59, and **Pressing**, page 60, to make quilt top. Work your way through the rows. Once each row is pieced it will be easy to put the quilt together. If you are using ombré fabrics, I encourage you to arrange all the pieces on a design wall so you can keep the ombré effect as you piece the quilt. Use ¹/₄" seam allowances throughout.*

Making Half-Squares Triangle (HST) Units
My preferred method for making half-squares triangles involves cutting the fabric a bit larger than necessary, sewing, pressing and trimming down to the correct size. No matter how much I'd like to think I can stitch a perfect quarter-inch seam, I can't. Making half-squares triangle units larger and squaring to the correct size ensures my accuracy.

I use the "Sew-First Method" for half-squares triangle units. This method creates 2 identical half-squares triangle units; even if only 1 unit is needed, I still make 2. This block is such a basic; it's always nice to have a small stash of them set aside for a future project.

Follow the instructions in each Row Assembly for which fabrics to pair for the HST units needed.

Tip: Use a tool like Clearly Perfect Angles by New Leaf Stitches.

1. Matching right side, place 2 squares 4" x 4" together. On the back of the lighter fabric, draw a line diagonally from corner to corner.

2. Stitch ¼" from each side of drawn line. Cut directly on the drawn line (**Fig. 1**).

Fig. 1

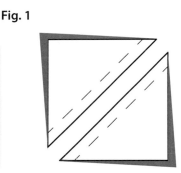

3. Open the units and press the seam allowances toward the darker fabric.

4. At this stage the unit will not be square. Trim the unit to 3½" x 3½" (**Fig. 2**).

Fig. 2

Corner Triangle Unit

This pattern has a few rectangular units that just need a single corner of color added to them. Follow the instructions in each Row Assembly for which fabrics to use for the Corner Triangle Units needed.

Left Corner Triangle Unit

1. On the back of a 3½" ombré fabric square, draw a line diagonal from corner to corner. Place the ombré fabric square on the upper left hand corner of a 6½" x 9½" rectangle. Stitch directly on the drawn line (**Fig. 3**).

Fig. 3

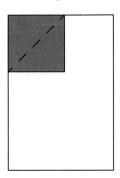

2. Trim ¼" from the stitching line. Press the seam allowances toward the ombré fabric (**Fig. 4**).

Fig. 4

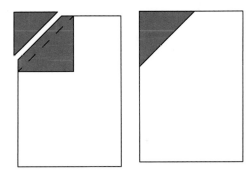

Right Corner Triangle Unit

1. On the back of a 3½" ombré fabric square, draw a line diagonal from corner to corner. Place the ombré fabric square on the upper right hand corner of a 6½" x 9½" rectangle. Stitch directly on the drawn line (**Fig. 5**).

Fig. 5

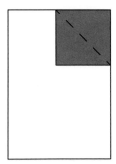

2. Trim ¹/₄" from the stitching line. Press the seam allowances toward the ombré fabric (**Fig. 6**).

Fig. 6

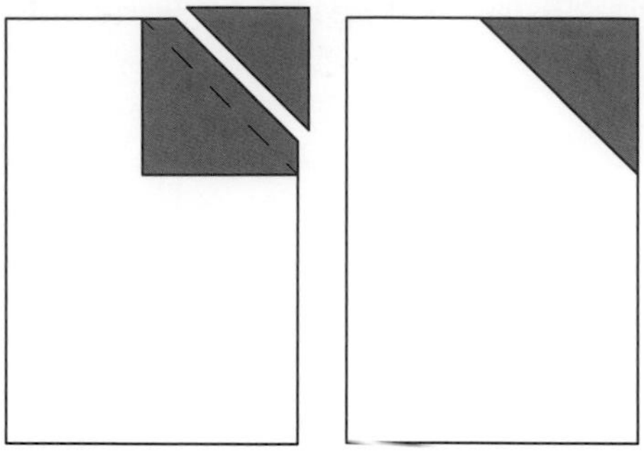

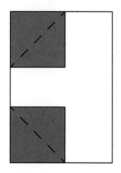

Double Left Corner Triangle Unit

1. On the back of two 3¹/₂" ombré fabric squares, draw a line diagonal from corner to corner. Place the ombré fabric squares on the upper left hand and lower left hand corners of a 6¹/₂" x 9¹/₂" rectangle. Stitch directly on the drawn line (**Fig. 7**).

Fig. 7

2. Trim ¹/₄" from each stitching line. Press the seam allowances toward the ombré fabric (**Fig. 8**).

Fig. 8

ROW ASSEMBLY
ROW A

1. Create 1 HST unit by pairing a 4" square of gray solid fabric #1 with a 4" square of hot pink fabric (**Fig. 9**). Trim to 3¹/₂" x 3¹/₂".

Fig. 9

2. Create 1 Left Corner Triangle Unit by pairing a 6¹/₂" x 9¹/₂" rectangle of gray solid fabric #1 with a 3¹/₂" square of mustard fabric (**Fig. 10**).

Fig. 10

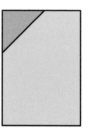

3. Create 1 Left Corner Triangle Unit by pairing a 6¹/₂" x 9¹/₂" rectangle of gray solid fabric #1 with a 3¹/₂" square of avocado fabric (**Fig. 11**).

Fig. 11

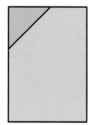

4. Refer to **Row A Diagrams** to lay out all gray solid fabric #1 pieces, six 3¹/₂" indigo squares, four 3¹/₂" purple squares, five 3¹/₂" hot pink squares, the HST unit, and both Left Corner Triangle Units.

5. Sew together columns of squares and HST as indicated. Press seam allowances as shown by arrows.

6. Continue to piece Row A together, pressing as shown by arrows.

ROW A DIAGRAMS

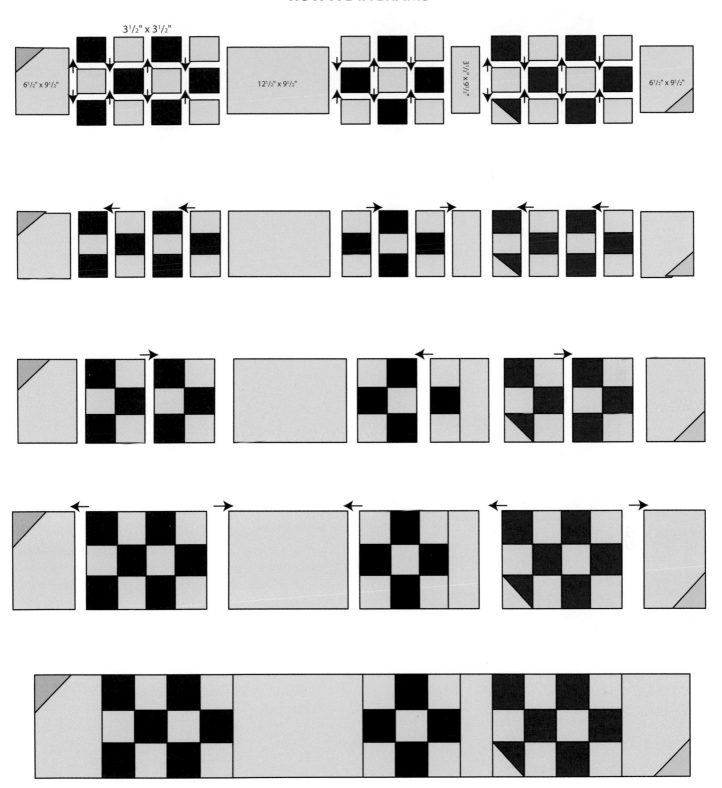

ROW B

1. Create 3 HST Units by pairing two 4" squares of gray solid fabric #2 with two 4" squares of hot pink fabric (**Fig. 12**). Trim to $3^1/_2$" x $3^1/_2$".

Fig. 12

2. Create 4 HST Units by pairing two 4" squares of gray solid fabric #2 with two 4" squares of avocado fabric (**Fig. 13**). Trim to $3^1/_2$" x $3^1/_2$".

Fig. 13

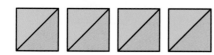

3. Create 1 Right Corner Triangle Unit by pairing a $6^1/_2$" x $9^1/_2$" rectangle of gray solid fabric #2 with a $3^1/_2$" square of mustard fabric (**Fig. 14**).

Fig. 14

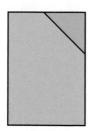

4. Create 1 Right Corner Triangle Unit by pairing a $6^1/_2$" x $9^1/_2$" rectangle of gray solid fabric #2 with a $3^1/_2$" square of avocado fabric (**Fig. 15**).

Fig. 15

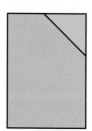

5. Refer to **Row B Diagrams** to lay out all the gray solid fabric #2 pieces with six $3^1/_2$" indigo squares, five $3^1/_2$" purple squares, one $3^1/_2$" hot pink squares, the HST units, and the Right Corner Triangle Units.

6. Sew together columns of squares and HST as indicated. Press seam allowances as shown by arrows.

7. Continue to piece Row B together, pressing as shown by arrows.

ROW B DIAGRAMS

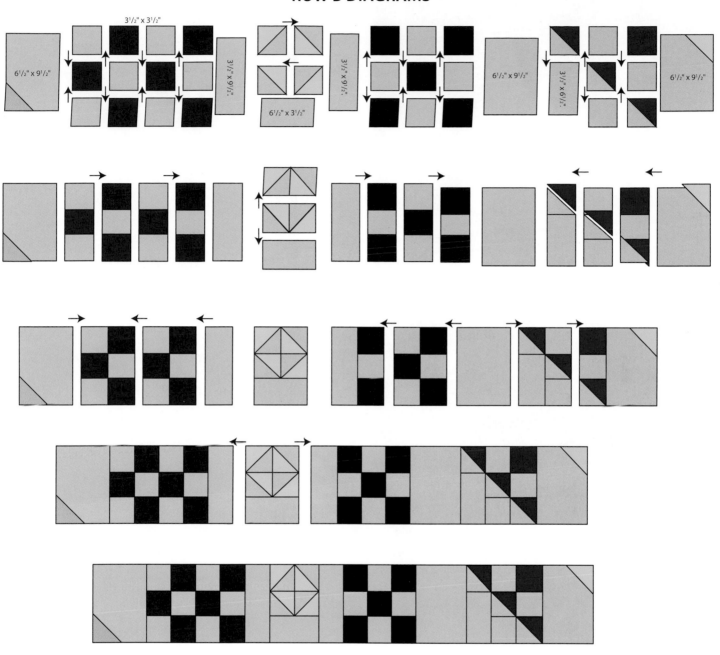

3. Create 3 HST Units by pairing two 4" squares of gray solid fabric #3 with two 4" squares of indigo fabric (**Fig. 18**). Trim to 3¹/₂" x 3¹/₂".

Fig. 18

4. Create 2 HST Units by pairing one 4" square of gray solid fabric #3 with one 4" square of persimmon fabric (**Fig. 19**). Trim to 3¹/₂" x 3¹/₂".

Fig. 19

5. Create one Double Left Corner Triangle Unit by pairing a 6¹/₂" x 9¹/₂" rectangle of gray solid fabric #3 with two 3¹/₂" squares of mustard fabric (**Fig. 20**).

Fig. 20

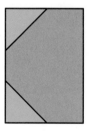

ROW C

1. Create 2 HST Units by pairing one 4" square of gray solid fabric #3 with one 4" square of magenta fabric (**Fig. 16**). Trim to 3¹/₂" x 3¹/₂".

Fig. 16

2. Create 4 HST Units by pairing two 4" squares of gray solid fabric #3 with two 4" squares of avocado fabric (**Fig. 17**). Trim to 3¹/₂" x 3¹/₂".

Fig. 17

6. Refer to **Row C Diagrams** to lay out all the gray solid fabric #3 pieces with two 3¹/₂" indigo squares, four 3¹/₂" purple squares, one 3¹/₂" magenta square, one 3¹/₂" persimmon square, the HST units, and the Double Left Corner Triangle Unit.

7. Sew together columns of squares and HST as indicated. Press seam allowances as shown by arrows.

8. Continue to piece Row C together, pressing as shown by arrows.

ROW C DIAGRAMS

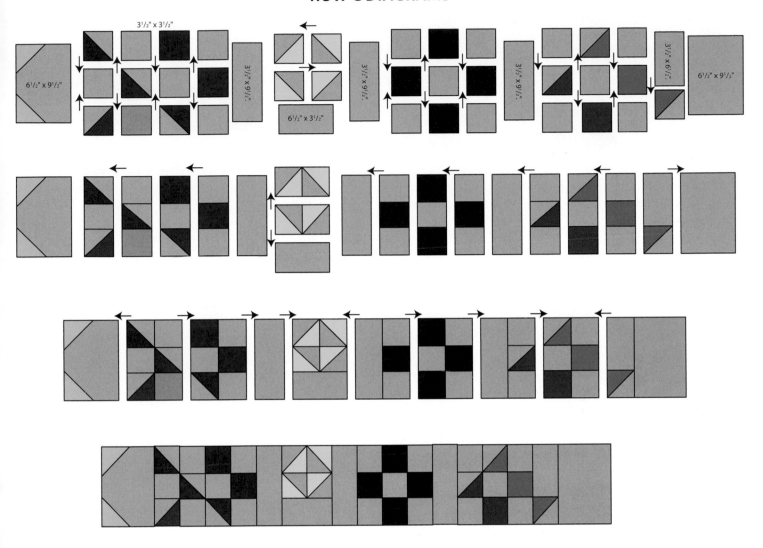

ROW D

1. Create 1 HST Unit by pairing one 4" square of gray solid fabric #4 with one 4" square of magenta fabric (**Fig. 21**). Trim to 3¹/₂" x 3¹/₂".

Fig. 21

2. Create 1 HST Unit by pairing one 4" square of gray solid fabric #4 with one 4" square of indigo fabric (**Fig. 22**). Trim to 3¹/₂" x 3¹/₂".

Fig. 22

3. Create 4 HST Units by pairing two 4" squares of gray solid fabric #3 with two 4" squares of avocado fabric (**Fig. 23**). Trim to 3¹/₂" x 3¹/₂".

Fig. 23

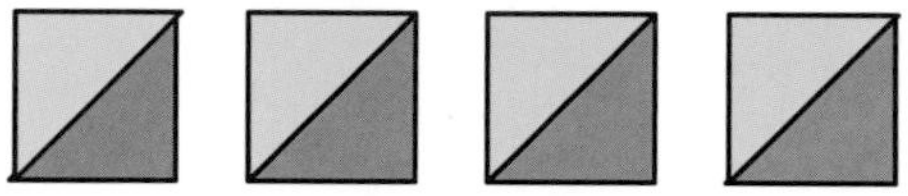

4. Create 6 HST Units by pairing three 4" squares of gray solid fabric #4 with three 4" squares of teal fabric (**Fig. 24**). Trim to 3¹/₂" x 3¹/₂".

Fig. 24

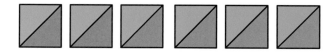

5. Create 3 HST Units by pairing two 4" squares of gray solid fabric #4 with two 4" squares of purple fabric (**Fig. 25**). Trim to 3¹/₂" x 3¹/₂".

Fig. 25

6. Create 3 HST Units by pairing two 4" squares of gray solid fabric #4 with two 4" squares of persimmon fabric (**Fig. 26**). Trim to 3¹/₂" x 3¹/₂".

Fig. 26

7. Create 1 Left Corner Triangle Unit by pairing a 6¹/₂" x 9¹/₂" rectangle of gray solid fabric #4 with a 3¹/₂" square of mustard fabric (**Fig. 27**)

Fig. 27

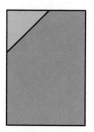

8. Create 1 Left Corner Triangle Unit by pairing a 6¹/₂" x 9¹/₂" rectangle of gray solid fabric #4 with a 3¹/₂" square of avocado fabric (**Fig. 28**).

Fig. 28

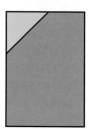

9. Refer to **Row D Diagrams** to lay out all the gray solid fabric #4 pieces with two 3¹/₂" magenta squares, one 3¹/₂" purple square, one 3¹/₂" persimmon square, the HST units, and the Left Corner Triangle Unit.

10. Sew together columns of squares and HST as indicated. Press seam allowances as shown by arrows.

11. Continue to piece Row D together, pressing as shown by arrows.

ROW D DIAGRAMS

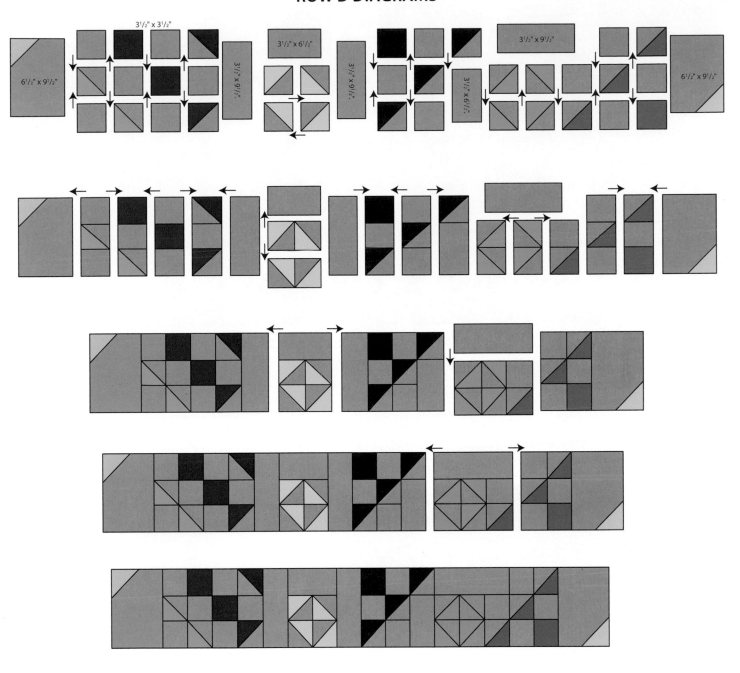

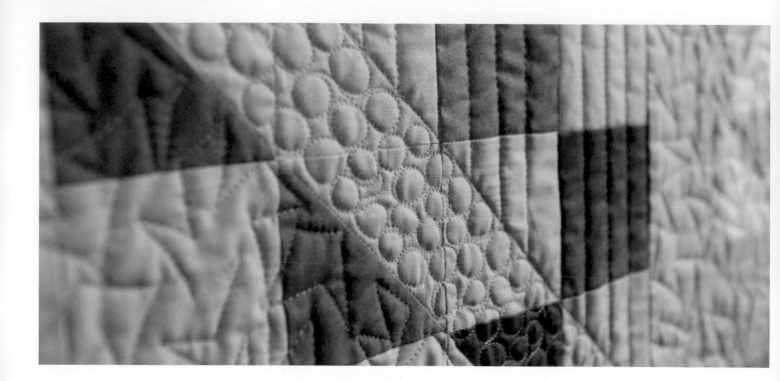

ROW E

1. Create 2 HST Units by pairing one 4" square of gray solid fabric #5 with one 4" square of teal fabric (**Fig. 29**). Trim to $3^1/2$" x $3^1/2$".

Fig. 29

2. Create 2 HST Units by pairing one 4" square of gray solid fabric #5 with one 4" square of mustard fabric (**Fig. 30**). Trim to $3^1/2$" x $3^1/2$".

Fig. 30

3. Create 1 HST Unit by pairing one 4" square of gray solid fabric #5 with one 4" square of persimmon fabric (**Fig. 31**). Trim to $3^1/2$" x $3^1/2$".

Fig. 31

4. Create 1 Right Corner Triangle Unit by pairing a $6^1/2$" x $9^1/2$" rectangle of gray solid fabric #5 with a $3^1/2$" square of avocado fabric (**Fig. 32**).

Fig. 32

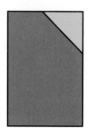

5. Refer to **Row E Diagrams** to lay out all the gray solid fabric #5 pieces with four $3^1/2$" teal squares, one $3^1/2$" mustard square, five $3^1/2$" persimmon squares, the HST units, and the Right Corner Triangle Unit.

6. Sew together columns of squares and HST as indicated. Press seam allowances as shown by arrows.

7. Continue to piece Row E together, pressing as shown by arrows.

ROW E DIAGRAMS

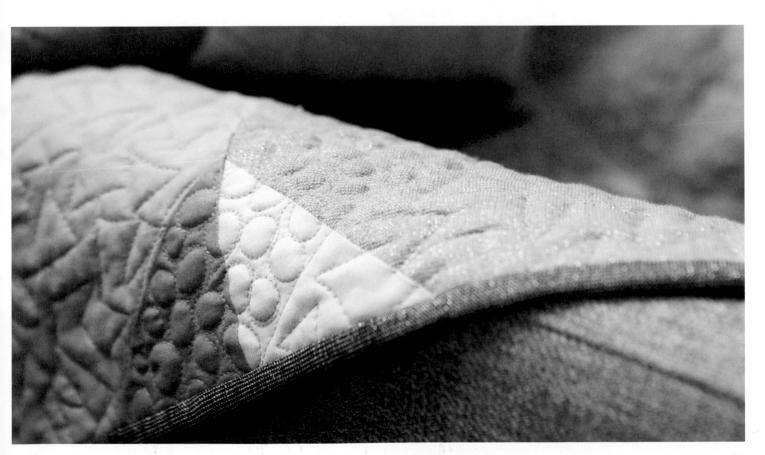

2. Create 3 HST Units by pairing two 4" squares of gray solid fabric #6 with two 4" squares of magenta fabric (**Fig. 34**). Trim to 3¹/₂" x 3¹/₂".

Fig. 34

3. Create 2 HST Units by pairing one 4" square of gray solid fabric #6 with one 4" square of persimmon fabric (**Fig. 35**). Trim to 3¹/₂" x 3¹/₂".

Fig. 35

4. Create 1 Right Corner Triangle Unit by pairing a 6¹/₂" x 9¹/₂" rectangle of gray solid fabric #6 with a 3¹/₂" square of mustard fabric (**Fig. 36**).

Fig. 36

ROW F

1. Create 4 HST Units by pairing two 4" squares of gray solid fabric #6 with two 4" squares of avocado fabric (**Fig. 33**). Two HST should be light and two should be dark. Trim to 3¹/₂" x 3¹/₂".

Fig. 33

5. Refer to **Row F Diagrams** to lay out all the gray solid fabric #6 pieces with six 3¹/₂" teal squares, one 3¹/₂" magenta square, four 3¹/₂" persimmon squares, the HST units, and the Right Corner Triangle Unit.

6. Sew together columns of squares and HST as indicated. Press seam allowances as shown by arrows.

7. Continue to piece Row F together, pressing as shown by arrows.

ROW F DIAGRAMS

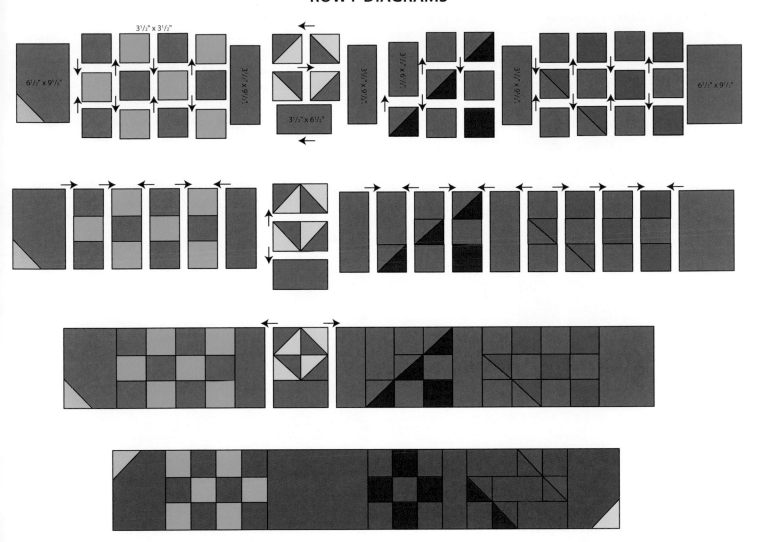

ROW G

1. Create 2 HST Units by pairing one 4" square of gray solid fabric #7 with one 4" square of hot pink fabric (**Fig. 37**). Trim to $3\frac{1}{2}$" x $3\frac{1}{2}$".

Fig. 37

2. Create 2 HST Units by pairing one 4" square of gray solid fabric #7 with one 4" square of persimmon fabric (**Fig. 38**). Trim to $3\frac{1}{2}$" x $3\frac{1}{2}$".

Fig. 38

3. Create 1 Left Corner Triangle Unit by pairing a $6\frac{1}{2}$" x $9\frac{1}{2}$" rectangle of gray solid fabric #7 with a $3\frac{1}{2}$" square of mustard fabric (**Fig. 39**).

Fig. 39

4. Create 1 Left Corner Triangle Unit by pairing a $6\frac{1}{2}$" x $9\frac{1}{2}$" rectangle of gray solid fabric #7 with a $3\frac{1}{2}$" square of avocado fabric (**Fig. 40**).

Fig. 40

5. Refer to **Row G Diagrams** to lay out all the gray solid fabric #7 pieces with six $3\frac{1}{2}$" teal squares, four $3\frac{1}{2}$" magenta squares, the HST units, and the Left Corner Triangle Units.

6. Sew together columns of squares and HST as indicated. Press seam allowances as shown by arrows.

7. Continue to piece Row G together, pressing as shown by arrows.

ROW G DIAGRAMS

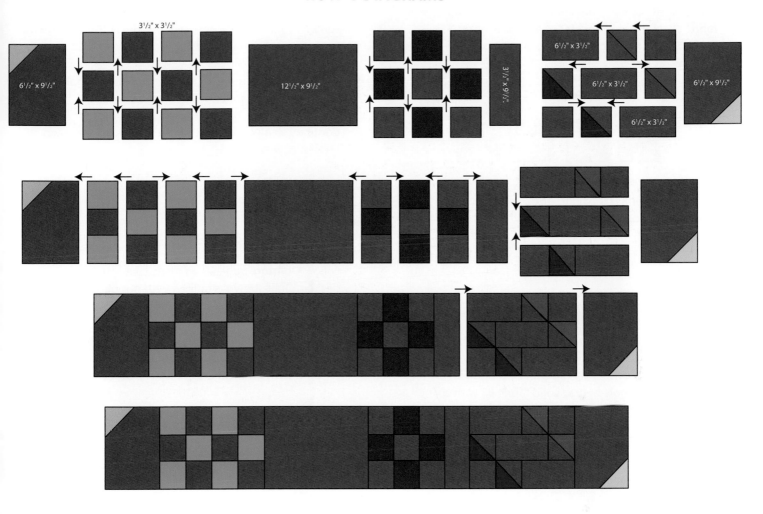

ROW H

1. Create 4 HST Units by pairing two 4" squares of gray solid fabric #8 with two 4" squares of avocado fabric (**Fig. 41**). Two HST should be light and two should be dark. Trim to $3^{1}/_{2}$" x $3^{1}/_{2}$".

Fig. 41

2. Create 2 HST Units by pairing one 4" square of gray solid fabric #8 with one 4" square of hot pink fabric (**Fig. 42**). Trim to $3^{1}/_{2}$" x $3^{1}/_{2}$".

Fig. 42

3. Create 1 Right Corner Triangle Unit by pairing a $6^{1}/_{2}$" x $9^{1}/_{2}$" rectangle of gray solid fabric #8 with a $3^{1}/_{2}$" square of mustard fabric (**Fig. 43**).

Fig. 43

4. Create 1 Right Corner Triangle Unit by pairing a $6^{1}/_{2}$" x $9^{1}/_{2}$" rectangle of gray solid fabric #8 with a $3^{1}/_{2}$" square of avocado fabric (**Fig. 44**).

Fig. 44

5. Refer to **Row H Diagrams** to lay out all the gray solid fabric #8 pieces with six $3^{1}/_{2}$" teal squares, five $3^{1}/_{2}$" magenta squares, four $3^{1}/_{2}$" hot pink squares, the HST units, and the Right Corner Triangle Units.

6. Sew together columns of squares and HST as indicated. Press seam allowances as shown by arrows.

7. Continue to piece Row H together, pressing as shown by arrows.

QUILT TOP ASSEMBLY

1. Refer to **Quilt Top Diagram** to sew Rows A-H together.

2. Follow **Quilting**, page 60, to mark, layer, and quilt as desired. Quilt shown is quilted with bubbles and straight and diagonal lines.

3. Use binding strips and follow **Making Straight-Grain Binding**, page 62, to make binding. Follow **Attaching Binding with Mitered Corners**, page 62, to bind quilt.

Quilt Top Diagram

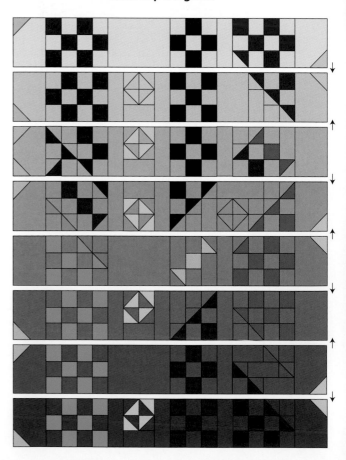

ROW H DIAGRAMS

MODERN HEXAGON MINI QUILT

DESIGN BY ALICIA STEELE

Adorn your table with this mini quilt. Perfect for the modern home.

Finished Quilt Size: 28³/4" x 23³/8" (73 cm x 59 cm)

SHOPPING LIST

Yardage is based on 43"/44" (109 cm/112 cm) wide fabric with a usable width of 40" (102 cm).

- ☐ ¹/2 yd (46 cm) of gray solid fabric
- ☐ ¹/2 yd (46 cm) of green solid fabric
- ☐ 1 yd (91 cm) of blue solid fabric
- ☐ 1 yd (91 cm) of pink solid fabric
- ☐ ⁷/8 yd (80 cm) of fabric for backing
- ☐ 3 yds (2.7 m) package of gray single-fold bias tape
- ☐ 30" x 50" (76 cm x 127 cm) piece of sew-in fleece

You will also need:

- ☐ walking foot for sewing machine
- ☐ paper
- ☐ pencil
- ☐ yard sticks
- ☐ dressmaker's tracing paper

MAKING THE PATTERN PIECES

All patterns include ¹/4" seam allowances.

1. Refer to **Fig. 1** and use the measurements given to draw a pattern on paper for the small triangle. Draw the stitching line ¹/4" inside the outer drawn line. At each point, draw a small dot where each stitching line intersects. Cut pattern from paper along outer drawn line.

2. Repeat Step 1 and refer to **Fig. 2** to make the large triangle pattern.

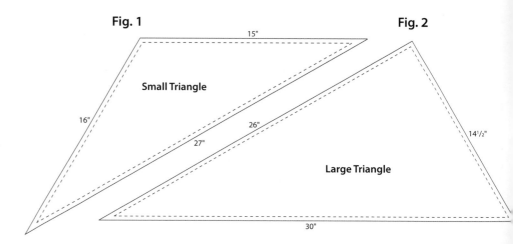

Fig. 1 — Small Triangle (15", 16", 27")
Fig. 2 — Large Triangle (26", 14¹/2", 30")

CUTTING THE PIECES

All patterns include ¹/4" seam allowances.

From gray solid fabric:
- Place pattern on **wrong** side of fabric and cut 1 **small triangle**. Use pencil and dressmaker's tracing paper to transfer dots to wrong side of fabric.

From green solid fabric:
- Place pattern on **right** side of fabric and cut 1 **small triangle**. Use pencil and dressmaker's tracing paper to transfer dots to wrong side of fabric.

From blue solid fabric:
- Place pattern on **right** side of fabric and cut 1 **large triangle**. Use pencil and dressmaker's tracing paper to transfer dots to wrong side of fabric.

From pink solid fabric:
- Place pattern on **wrong** side of fabric and cut 1 **large triangle**. Use pencil and dressmaker's tracing paper to transfer dots to wrong side of fabric.

MAKING THE QUILT

*Follow **Piecing**, page 59, and **Pressing**, page 60, to make quilt top. Match right sides of fabric and use $1/4$" seam allowances throughout.*

1. Matching the dots, sew the large triangles together along the long edge. Press seam allowances open.
2. Matching the dots, sew 1 small triangle to remaining edges of large triangles. Press seam allowances towards small triangles (**Fig. 3**).

Fig. 3

COMPLETING THE QUILT

1. Cut 2 layers of fleece approximately $1/2$" larger on all sides than the quilt top.

2. Follow **Quilting**, page 60, to mark, layer, and quilt (using walking foot) as desired. Quilt shown is quilted in straight lines radiating from the point.

3. Trim the excess fleece even with the quilt top edges.

4. Use the quilted top as a pattern to cut the backing fabric. Matching wrong sides, layer the quilted top on the backing. Baste $1/8$" from raw edges.

5. Unfold the bias tape. Press 1 short end $1/4$" to wrong side. Beginning with pressed end, pin 1 long edge of the tape along the raw edge of the quilt top on the backing side. Refer to **Attaching Binding with Mitered Corners**, page 62, Steps 2 - 6 to stitch bias tape in place $1/4$" from raw edges. When you reach the beginning end, overlap the tape about 1" and trim.

6. Pin the folded edge of the binding to the front of the quilt top. Mitering corners, sew in place using the sewing machine or by hand sewing.

SQUARE-IN-A-SQUARE COASTER

DESIGN BY CAROLINA MOORE

Add some modern flair to your living space with these quilt-as-you-go modern coasters. Simple to make from scraps left over from another project in the book. I used leftover fabrics from the Square Dance Quilt. You can make a few or make stacks to give as gifts!

Finished Coaster Size: 3½" x 3½" (9 cm x 9 cm)

SHOPPING LIST

Yardage is based on 43"/44" (109 cm/112 cm) wide fabric with a usable width of 40" (102 cm) and will make 1 coaster.

☐ assorted scraps of fabrics
☐ 2½" x 20" (6 cm x 51 cm) piece of fabric for binding
☐ 5" x 5" (13 cm x 13 cm) square of fabric for backing

You will also need:

☐ 5" x 5" (13 cm x 13 cm) piece of batting (You can use 2 squares if a thicker coaster is desired.)
☐ water-soluble marking pen (optional)

CUTTING THE PIECES

*Follow **Rotary Cutting**, page 58, to cut fabric. Cut all strips from the selvage-to-selvage width of the fabric. All measurements include ¼" seam allowances.*

From assorted fabrics:

- Cut 1 **square** 2" x 2" for center.
- Cut 2 squares 1⅞" x 1⅞". Cut each square in half diagonally to make 4 **small triangles**.
- Cut 2 squares 2⅞" x 2⅞". Cut each square in half diagonally to make 4 **large triangles**.

MAKING THE COASTER

*Follow **Piecing**, page 59, and **Pressing**, page 60, to make coaster. Use ¼" seam allowances throughout.*

1. Place the backing fabric right side down. Place the batting square(s) on top of the backing. Center the **square** in the center of the batting. Matching right sides, align the long edge of 1 **small triangle** along 1 edge of the square. Stitch ¼" from the edges, starting on 1 edge of the batting and extending across to the opposite edge (**Fig. 1**). If needed, you can draw a line with a water-soluble marker first as a stitching guide. Finger press the triangle open.

Fig. 1

2. Repeat Step 1, adding a small triangle on the opposite edge, and then small triangles on the 2 remaining edges (**Fig. 2**).

3. Repeat Steps 1-2, adding the **large triangles (Fig. 3)**.

4. Trim the square to 3½" x 3½".

5. Use binding strips and follow **Making Straight-Grain Binding**, page 62, to make binding. Follow **Attaching Binding with Mitered Corners**, page 62, to bind coaster.

Fig. 2

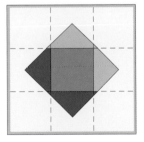

Fig. 3

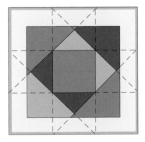

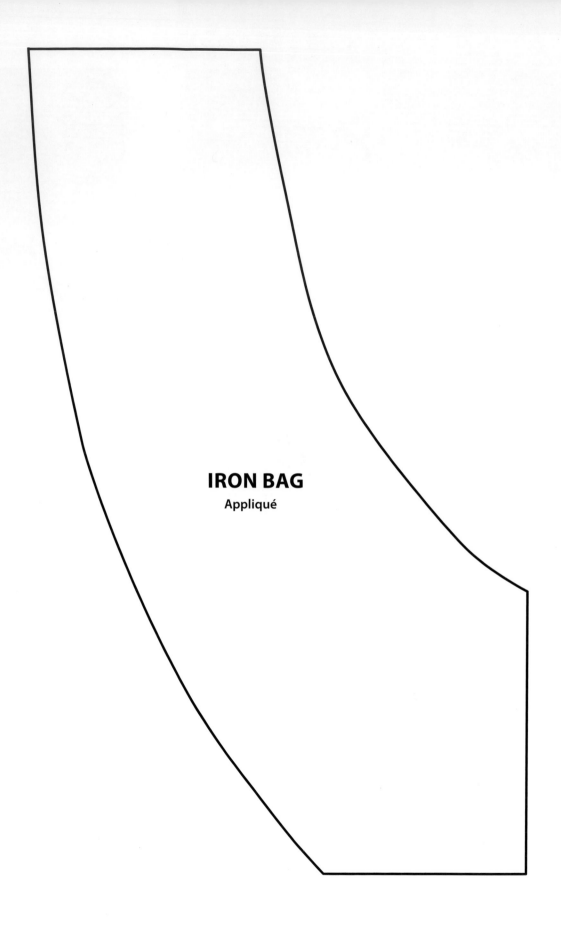

IRON BAG

Appliqué

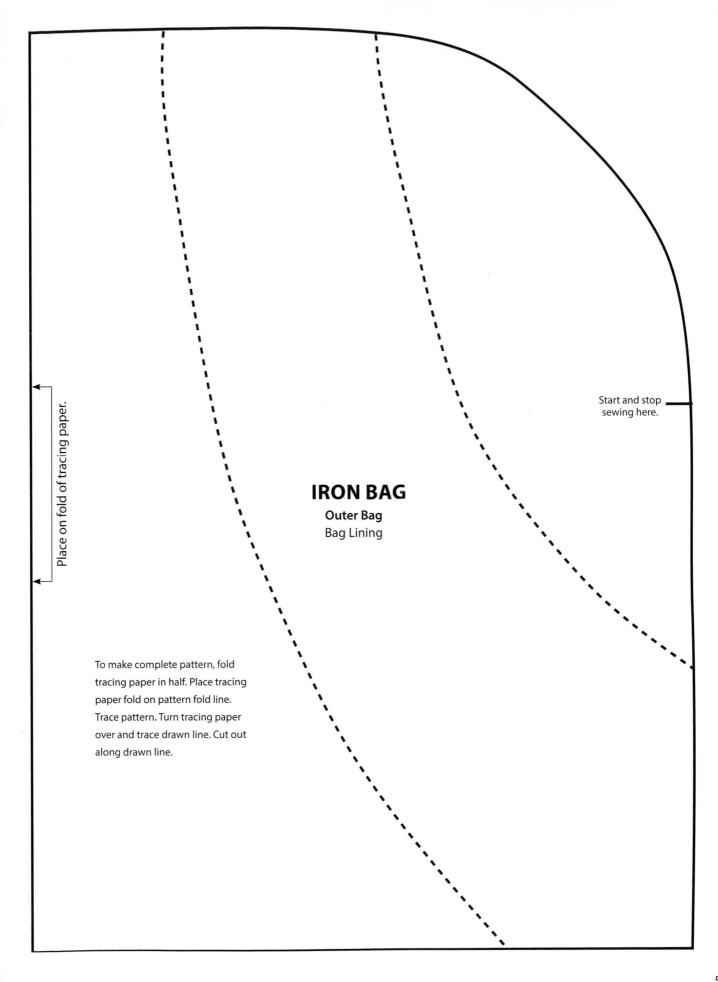

Place on fold of tracing paper.

Start and stop sewing here.

IRON BAG

Outer Bag
Bag Lining

To make complete pattern, fold tracing paper in half. Place tracing paper fold on pattern fold line. Trace pattern. Turn tracing paper over and trace drawn line. Cut out along drawn line.

GENERAL INSTRUCTIONS

To make your sewing easier and more enjoyable, we encourage you to carefully read all of the general instructions, study the color photographs, and familiarize yourself with the individual project instructions before beginning a project.

FABRICS

SELECTING FABRICS
Choose high-quality, medium-weight 100% cotton fabrics. All-cotton fabrics hold a crease better and fray less.

Yardage requirements listed for each project are based on 43"/44" wide fabric with a "usable" width of 40" after shrinkage and trimming selvages. Actual usable width will probably vary slightly from fabric to fabric. Our recommended yardage lengths should be adequate for occasional re-squaring of the fabric when many cuts are required.

PREPARING FABRICS
Pre-washing fabrics may cause edges to ravel. As a result, your precut fabrics may not be large enough to cut all of the pieces required for your chosen projects. Therefore, we do not recommend pre-washing yardage or precut fabrics.

Before cutting, prepare fabrics with a steam iron set on cotton and starch or sizing. The starch or sizing will give the fabric a crisp finish. This will make cutting more accurate and may make piecing easier.

We recommend that all fabrics be washed, dried, and pressed before cutting. If fabrics are not pre-washed, washing the finished quilt will cause shrinkage and give it a more "antiqued" look and feel. Bright and dark colors, which may run, should always be washed before cutting. After washing and drying fabric,

ROTARY CUTTING

CUTTING FROM YARDAGE
- Fold the fabric lengthwise with wrong sides together and matching selvages.

- Place fabric on work surface with fold closest to you.

- Cut all strips from the selvage-to-selvage width of the fabric unless otherwise indicated in the project instructions.

- Square the left edge of the fabric using a rotary cutter and rulers (**Figs. 1-2**).

- To cut each strip required for a project, place the ruler over the cut edge of the fabric, aligning the desired marking on the ruler with the cut edge; make the cut (**Fig. 3**).

- When cutting several strips from a single piece of fabric, it is important to make sure that the cuts remain at a perfect right angle to the fold; square the fabric as needed.

CUTTING FROM PRECUTS
- Many precut fabrics have pinked edges and most manufacturers include the points of the pinked edges in the measurement given on the label. Before cutting precuts into smaller pieces, measure your precuts to determine if you need to include the points to achieve the correct cut size.

- If cutting strips parallel to the long edge, place fat quarter on work surface with short edge closest to you. Cut all strips parallel to the long edge of the fabric in the same manner as cutting from yardage unless otherwise indicated in project instructions.

- To cut each strip, place ruler over cut edge of fabric, aligning desired marking on ruler with cut edge; make cut.

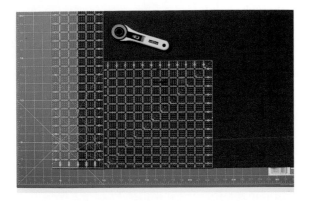

Fig. 1

Fig. 2

Fig. 3

PIECING

Precise cutting, followed by accurate piecing/sewing, will ensure that all pieces fit together well.

- Set the sewing machine stitch length for approximately 11 stitches per inch.

- Use neutral-colored general-purpose sewing thread (not quilting thread) in the needle and in the bobbin.

- An accurate seam allowance is *essential*.

- When piecing/sewing, always place the pieces right sides together and match the raw edges; pin if necessary.

- Trim away the points of seam allowances that extend beyond the edges of the sewn pieces.

SEWING ACROSS SEAM INTERSECTIONS

When sewing across intersection of two seams, place pieces right sides together and match seams exactly, making sure seam allowances are pressed in opposite directions (**Fig. 4**).

Fig. 4

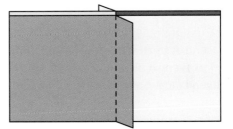

SEWING SHARP POINTS

To ensure sharp points when joining triangular or diagonal pieces, stitch across the center of the "X" (shown in pink) formed on wrong side by previous seams (**Fig. 5**).

Fig. 5

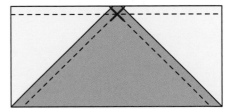

PRESSING

- Use a steam iron set on "Cotton" for all pressing.

- Press after sewing each seam.

- Seam allowances are almost always pressed to 1 side, usually toward the darker fabric. However, to reduce bulk it may occasionally be necessary to press the seam allowances toward the lighter fabric or even to press them open.

- To prevent a dark fabric seam allowance from showing through a light fabric, trim the darker seam allowance slightly narrower than the lighter seam allowance.

QUILTING

*Quilting holds the three layers (top, batting, and backing) of the quilt together and can be done by hand or machine. Because marking, layering, and quilting are interrelated and may be done in different orders depending on the circumstances, please read the entire **Quilting** section, pages 60-61, before beginning the project.*

MARKING QUILTING LINES

Quilting lines may be marked using fabric marking pencils, chalk markers, or water- or air-soluble pens.

Simple quilting designs may be marked with chalk or chalk pencil after basting. A small area may be marked, then quilted, before moving to the next area to be marked. Intricate designs should be marked before basting using a more durable marker.

Caution: Pressing may permanently set some marks. **Test** different markers **on scrap fabric** to find one that marks clearly and can be thoroughly removed.

PREPARING THE BACKING

To allow for slight shifting of the quilt top during quilting, the backing should be approximately 4" larger on all sides. Yardage requirements listed for quilt backings are calculated for 43"/44"w fabric. Using 90"w or 108"w fabric for the backing of a bed-sized quilt may eliminate piecing. To piece a backing using 43"/44"w fabric, use the following instructions.

1. Measure the length and width of the quilt top; add 8" to each measurement.

2. If the determined width is 79" or less, cut the backing fabric into 2 lengths slightly longer than the determined *length* measurement. Trim the selvages. Place the lengths with right sides facing and sew the long edges together, forming a tube (**Fig. 6**). Match the seams and press along one fold (**Fig. 7**). Cut along the pressed fold to form a single piece (**Fig. 8**).

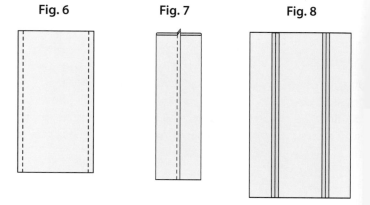

Fig. 6   Fig. 7   Fig. 8

3. Trim the backing to the size determined in Step 1; press the seam allowances open.

CHOOSING THE BATTING

The appropriate batting will make quilting easier. For fine hand quilting, choose low-loft batting. All cotton or cotton/polyester blend battings work well for machine quilting because the cotton helps "grip" quilt layers. If the quilt is to be tied, a high-loft batting, sometimes called extra-loft or fat batting, may be used to make the quilt "fluffy."

Types of batting include cotton, polyester, wool, cotton/polyester blend, cotton/wool blend, and silk.

When selecting batting, refer to the package labels for characteristics and care instructions. Cut the batting the same size as the prepared backing.

ASSEMBLING THE QUILT

1. Examine the wrong side of the quilt top closely; trim any seam allowances and clip any threads that may show through the front of the quilt. Press the quilt top, being careful not to "set" any marked quilting lines.

2. Place the backing *wrong* side up on flat surface. Use masking tape to tape the edges of the backing to the surface. Place the batting on top of the backing fabric. Smooth the batting gently, being careful not to stretch or tear. Center the quilt top *right* side up on the batting.

3. Use 1" rustproof safety pins to "pin-baste" all layers together, spacing the pins approximately 4" apart. Begin at the center and work toward outer edges to secure all the layers. If possible, place pins away from the areas that will be quilted, although the pins may be removed as needed when quilting.

MACHINE QUILTING METHODS

Use general-purpose thread in the bobbin. Do not use quilting thread. Thread the needle of machine with general-purpose thread or transparent monofilament thread to make the quilting blend with the quilt top fabrics. Use decorative thread, such as a metallic or contrasting-color general-purpose thread, to make the quilting lines stand out more.

Straight-Line Quilting

The term "straight-line" is somewhat deceptive, since curves (especially gentle ones) as well as straight lines can be stitched with this technique.

1. Set the stitch length for six to ten stitches per inch and attach the walking foot to the sewing machine.

2. Determine which section of the quilt will have the longest continuous quilting line, oftentimes the area from the center top to the center bottom. Roll up and secure each edge of the quilt to help reduce the bulk, keeping the fabrics smooth. Smaller projects may not need to be rolled.

3. Begin stitching on the longest quilting line, using very short stitches for the first $1/4$" to "lock" quilting. Stitch across the project, using one hand on each side of the walking foot to slightly spread the fabric and to guide the fabric through the machine. Lock the stitches at end of the quilting line.

4. Continue machine quilting, stitching longer quilting lines first to stabilize quilt before moving on to other areas.

Free-Motion Quilting

Free-motion quilting may be free form or may follow a marked pattern.

1. Attach the darning foot to the sewing machine and lower or cover the feed dogs.

2. Position the quilt under the darning foot; lower the foot. Holding the top thread, take a stitch and pull the bobbin thread to top of quilt. To "lock" the beginning of the quilting line, hold the top and bobbin threads while making three to five stitches in place.

3. Use one hand on each side of the darning foot to slightly spread the fabric and to move the fabric through the machine. Even stitch length is achieved by using smooth, flowing hand motion and steady machine speed. Slow machine speed and fast hand movement will create long stitches. Fast machine speed and slow hand movement will create short stitches. Move quilt sideways, back and forth, in a circular motion, or in a random motion to create the desired designs; do not rotate the quilt. Lock stitches at the end of each quilting line.

BINDING

MAKING STRAIGHT-GRAIN BINDING

1. Cut lengthwise or crosswise strips of binding fabric the determined length and width called for in the project instructions.

2. To piece binding strips, use the diagonal seams method (**Fig. 9**).

Fig. 9

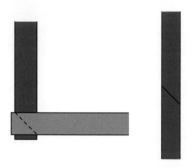

3. Matching the wrong sides and raw edges, press the strip(s) in half lengthwise to complete the binding.

ATTACHING BINDING WITH MITERED CORNERS

1. Beginning with one end near the center on the bottom edge of the quilt, lay the binding around the quilt to make sure that the seams in the binding will not end up at a corner. Adjust placement if necessary. Matching the raw edges of the binding to the raw edge of the quilt top, pin the binding to the right side of the quilt along one edge.

2. When you reach the first corner, mark ¹/₄" from the corner of the quilt top (**Fig. 10**).

Fig. 10

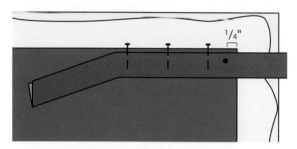

3. Beginning approximately 10" from the end of the binding and using a ¹/₄" seam allowance, sew the binding to the quilt, backstitching at the beginning of stitching and at the mark (**Fig. 11**). Lift the needle out of the fabric and clip the thread.

Fig. 11

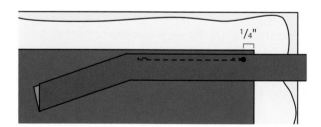

4. Fold the binding as shown in **Figs. 12-13** and pin the binding to the adjacent side, matching the raw edges. When you've reached the next corner, mark 1/4" from the edge of the quilt top.

Fig. 12

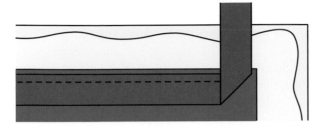

Fig. 13

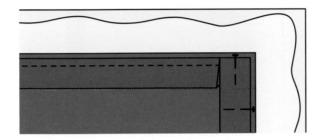

5. Backstitching at the edge of quilt top, sew the pinned binding to the quilt **(Fig. 14)**; backstitch at the next mark. Lift the needle out of the fabric and clip the thread.

Fig. 14

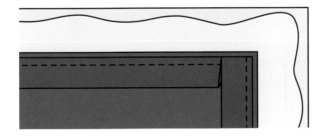

6. Continue sewing the binding to the quilt, stopping approximately 10" from the starting point **(Fig. 15)**.

7. Bring the beginning and end of the binding to the center of the opening and fold each end back, leaving a 1/4" space between the folds **(Fig. 16)**. Finger press the folds.

Fig. 15   **Fig. 16**

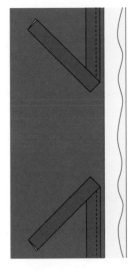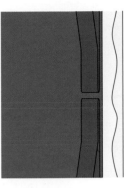

8. Unfold the ends of the binding and draw a line across the wrong side in the finger-pressed crease. Draw a line through the lengthwise pressed fold of binding at the same spot to create a cross mark. With the edge of the ruler at the cross mark, line up the 45° angle marking on the ruler with one long side of the binding. Draw a diagonal line from edge to edge. Repeat on the remaining end, making sure that the 2 diagonal lines are angled the same way **(Fig. 17)**.

Fig. 17

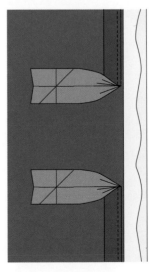

9. Matching the right sides and diagonal lines, pin the binding ends together at right angles (**Fig. 18**).

10. Machine stitch along the diagonal line (**Fig. 19**), removing the pins as you stitch.

11. Lay the binding against the quilt to double check that it is correct length.

12. Trim the binding ends, leaving a ¹/₄" seam allowance; press the seam allowances open. Stitch the binding to the quilt.

13. Trim the backing and batting a scant ¹/₄" larger than the quilt top so that the batting and backing will fill the binding when it is folded over to the quilt backing.

14. On one edge of the quilt, fold the binding over to the quilt backing and pin the pressed edge in place, covering the stitching line (**Fig. 20**). On the adjacent side, fold the binding over, forming a mitered corner (**Fig. 21**). Repeat to pin the remainder of the binding in place.

15. Blindstitch the binding to the backing, taking care not to stitch through to the quilt front.

Fig. 18

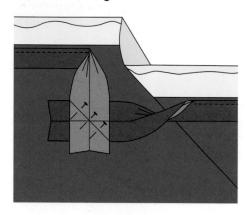

Fig. 20

Fig. 21

Fig. 19

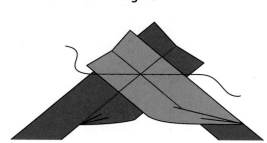

Production Team: Senior Graphic Artist - Lora Puls; Graphic Artist - Erin P. Lang; Photographer - Jason Masters; and Photography Stylist – Lori Wenger.

We have made every effort to ensure that these instructions are accurate and complete. We cannot, however, be responsible for human error, typographical mistakes, or variations in individual work.

Made in U.S.A..

Library of Congress Control Number: 2019938047.